ILLUSTRATED
HISTORY of
NEW ZEALAND

ILLUSTRATED HISTORY of NEW ZEALAND

Marcia Stenson

RANDOM HOUSE
NEW ZEALAND

National Library of New Zealand Cataloguing-in-Publication Data
Stenson, Marcia.
Illustrated history of New Zealand / Marcia Stenson.
Includes index.
ISBN-13: 978 1 86941 602 7
1. New Zealand—History—Juvenile literature. I. Title.
993—dc 21

A RANDOM HOUSE BOOK
published by
Random House New Zealand
18 Poland Rd, Glenfield, Auckland, New Zealand

www.randomhouse.co.nz

This edition first published 2004, reprinted 2004, 2006, 2007, 2008

ISBN-13: 978 1 86941 602 7

Picture research: Nicola McCloy
Design: Sharon Grace, Grace Design
Front cover illustrations: top left and right, bottom left, Alexander Turnbull Library;
middle left, Fairfax Sundays; middle right, Te Papa Tongarewa.
Back cover illustrations: top left, Natural Sciences Image Library; top middle and right,
Alexander Turnbull Library; bottom, Te Papa Tongarewa
Printed in China

CONTENTS

How we know about the past

We get most of what we know about the past from three places:

1. ARCHAEOLOGY

Archaeologists look at the physical evidence. They try to understand how people lived and how the world around them affected their lives. Archaeologists want to know how humans organised themselves.

What we can't know is how accurate archaeologists are. Have they found all the physical evidence left behind by our ancestors? Will they develop better techniques for working out how old the things they find are? Based on the evidence they think they know how people lived — have they got it right?

Artefacts such as this fish hook (above right), mere (club), pounamu adze and kotiate (hand club) help archaeologists to understand how people lived in the past.

2. ORAL TRADITIONS

Stories are passed on from generation to generation without being written down. We never know how much is accurate, how much is exaggeration or how much has been missed out.

Sometimes we can get confirmation from another source. The Maori traditions about arrival in Aotearoa tell of planned voyages. Scientists and historians who have studied the ocean currents and looked at the evidence agree — Polynesian discoveries of new lands were not accidental or the result of drifting.

3. WRITTEN RECORDS

These are things people have written in the past. We can see this evidence for ourselves. But we don't know how reliable it is. We have to ask ourselves who recorded the event. Did they see it themselves or did someone tell them about it? Have we got the whole truth? Would someone else who was there have a different story to tell?

A good example of this is the signing of the Treaty of Waitangi. We have a record of what happened written by Pakeha but we do not have a record written by Maori. Would they have seen things differently?

Above: Sir Apirana Ngata speaks at Raukawa Marae in Otaki.

We have to use all these sources of information. We have to check one off against the other when we can. We have to make a few guesses but be ready to think again when new evidence appears.

Below: The people on this list all travelled on the RMS *Ruahine*. Written records like this help us to learn about our history.

Above: The Waitangi sheet of the Treaty of Waitangi is a good example of how written records help us to know about history. This is one of seven copies of the Treaty that were sent around the country for signing. The sheet has been rescued from a fire, wet in a flood and was nibbled on by mice. It is now being well looked after by the specialists at National Archives. Also see pages 34–37 for more information about the Treaty.

Land of birds

Of places in the world where humans could live comfortably, New Zealand was the last settled. For about 80 million years, trees, birds, frogs, reptiles and insects had New Zealand to themselves.

In an isolated land, over millions of years, they adapted. The wings of some birds became smaller and smaller until, like the kiwi and the moa, they could not fly at all. Some developed features not found elsewhere, like New Zealand geckos and skinks, which give birth to live young instead of laying eggs.

FOREST BIRDS

Giant trees in podocarp and beech forests were home to many birds. Some, like the tiny wrens, were ancient species. Living in the high treetops was the huia (*Heteralocha acutirostris*), a beautiful, glossy black bird with orange wattles on its throat, a bit larger than a magpie. The female's beak was long and curved, the male's was short and stouter. There was the native thrush or piopio (*Turnagra*

Above: Flightless birds like the takahe roamed the grasslands and the forest floors.

Top left: A male huia.

Below: The native thrush, piopio, lived high in the trees.

capensis). Among the predators, which attacked other birds, were varieties of morepork. But the biggest predator was the great eagle (*Harpagnornis moorei*). It had a wing span of between 2 and 3 metres, weighed from 9 to 13 kilograms and was the largest eagle in the world. A fierce hunter, it would even attack the huge moa. Maori legends tell of the Pouakai, a great bird that attacked children and adults. The Pouakai, probably the great eagle, was killed by the warrior Te Hau o Tawera.

The unusual adzebill (*Aptornis otidiforms*) was one of the birds that lived on the forest floor. It could not fly, stood 80 centimetres high and weighed up to 10 kilograms. It used its strong neck and huge beak to smash open logs for grubs. The kakapo (the world's largest parrot), weka and kaka were the most common birds after the moa.

Above left: Forests of giant trees covered the land.

Top: The cheeky kaka, which is a native parrot, was one of the most common birds.

Above: The weka, an inquisitive flightless bird, was also very commonly found.

Right: In the high tree-tops was the huia, whose beautiful feathers were later much sought after by Maori chiefs. This is a female huia.

MOA

The moa roamed everywhere. There were 30 moa per square kilometre (today there are about 10 humans per square kilometre). A dozen species of moa lived in New Zealand. All had small heads, long necks, long legs and no wings. The largest was 1.6 metres high at the hips and weighed 200 to 300 kilograms. It probably carried its neck in a relaxed 'S' pose to make it easier to push through the thick forest. It could reach up 3 metres to feed. The smallest moa were about 70 centimetres high at the hips and about 20 to 30 kilograms in weight.

Moa dominated New Zealand for millions of years. Their feeding kept the bush floor open. They helped spread seeds. They may even

Above: The giant moa dominated the land.

Right: The juvenile lancewood (*Pseudopanax crassifolius*) has long, leathery, downward-facing leaves, thought to have evolved as protection against moa.

have been responsible for so many New Zealand plants having tough, leathery inedible leaves when they are young. Once these plants get to 4 metres tall (out of reach of moa) they have delicate, tasty little leaves. Even today, on farming land, you can see tracks zigzagging down the hillsides where once moa made their way through thick bush.

Above: The tuatara was the only survivor of an ancient group of animals which lived at the same time as the dinosaurs.

Above: The giant weta used its spiky hind legs for defence.

Above: Hochstetter's frog (*Leiopelma hochstetteri*) is a primitive native frog which was once very common.

Below: Skinks were abundant throughout New Zealand.

OTHER CREATURES

The tuatara was the only survivor of an ancient group of animals. New Zealand is the only place where they did not become extinct when the dinosaurs did. The giant gecko (*Hoplodactylus delcourti*), called kawekaweau, was 60 centimetres long and as thick as a man's wrist. Brown with dull red stripes, it was found throughout the North Island. Skinks, frogs and large insects like the weta abounded. But it was a land ruled by birds.

Many of these creatures, such as the moa, the huia, the great eagle and the giant gecko, are now extinct. Others are endangered species.

Key points about pre-human NZ
- For 80 million years birds, reptiles and insects had New Zealand to themselves.
- When humans came, the creatures were hunted and their environment was destroyed.
- Many like the moa, the huia, the giant eagle and the adzebill became extinct.
- Others like the takahe and the kiwi survive only in protected areas.

Arrival of the Maori

About 6000 years ago a group of people began to move
eastwards from south-east Asia. They travelled in outrigger
canoes with pigs, dogs, rats, chickens and some root and tree
crops. They could carve wood, build houses and make pottery,
and were good at fishing.

NAVIGATING THE PACIFIC

Above all they were very good long-distance
sailors, using a 'star compass' to check the
position of the stars. During the day they
watched the ocean, the way swells formed
patterns as they bounced off islands, the sea
creatures found in different waters, the islands,
reefs, sandbanks and areas of rough water.
The navigator slept as little as possible. He
was the one with bloodshot eyes, scanning the
sea and the night sky, keeping watch for birds
and land clouds, watching for floating
coconuts, seaweed or driftwood that might
show that land was nearby.

Top: Double-hulled canoes were more stable in rough
weather and had more room for supplies. This picture was
drawn by Isaac Gilsemans who came to New Zealand
with Abel Tasman in 1642.

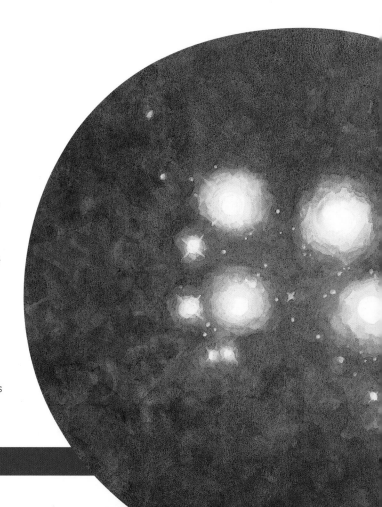

Above: In his painting 'The Arrival of the Maori' C.F. Goldie shows us his interpretation of what was almost certainly a hard and dangerous journey.

CANOES

Outrigger or double canoes were about 15 to 25 metres long. They were fast, sailing at about 4 to 7 knots (7 to 13 kilometres per hour), or more in a good wind. They could easily cover 160 kilometres in a day, and could carry 40 to 50 people. On long journeys the travellers took with them food, water, animals and plants, as well as personal possessions.

EXPLORATION

These people planned voyages to explore and find new lands in which to live, and improved their sailing skills as they went. The further they went the more different they became from the people their ancestors had left behind. They became Polynesian.

The big gap between Rarotonga and New Zealand held up their explorations and settlement. Not until some time between AD 800 and AD 1350 did the Polynesians reach New Zealand, the last place on earth where people could live.

A PLANNED JOURNEY

They were not blown off course. Ocean currents would have taken them in other directions. With them they had dogs, food plants such as kumara, taro, hue (gourds) and yam — and rats. The voyage took between two weeks and a month. With rough seas and wild winds, many would have been lost at sea. Recent DNA research has shown that all Maori are descended from a founding population of 50 to 100 women. They could not have all fitted on one or two canoes, even double ones. This agrees with the Maori tradition of a number of canoes setting out. They may have sailed weeks, months or years apart.

Some voyagers may even have returned home to pass on sailing directions or to collect food plants, though with prevailing winds and strong currents this would have been more

Left: Matariki is a cluster of seven stars which would have been important for navigation. Matariki is also known as the Pleiades or the Seven Sisters.

Above: Hue, or gourds, were brought to New Zealand by early Maori. They were used not only as food but also as vessels for water.

difficult than the trip to New Zealand.

Maori legends tell of planned voyages, usually after quarrels about land or women. Other legends claim Maori are descended from an ancestor who had always lived in Aotearoa.

LEGENDS

All the different legends celebrate the arrival of Maori ancestors in a new place. Later, when the first settled areas became overcrowded, they made voyages within New Zealand. One group who settled the Chatham Islands became known as the Moriori. Perhaps these new voyagers called their canoes after the ancient ones that brought them to Aotearoa. We don't know which parts of the legends about the great canoe voyages of Aotea, Te Arawa, Kurahaupo, Mataatua, Tainui, Takitimu and Tokomaru refer to voyages to New Zealand, and which parts refer to voyages around New Zealand.

Above: Some legends say that the explorer Kupe tracked the shining cuckoo to find the route to Aotearoa and that he passed on sailing directions for others to follow him.

ARRIVAL

We cannot be sure exactly when the voyagers arrived. Sometime between AD 1300 and AD 1390 a volcano near Tarawera erupted. Its ash covered large regions of the North Island and there are no signs left by humans underneath. But under the ash of later eruptions, such as those of Rangitoto and Taranaki between AD 1400 and AD 1450, there are signs of human presence.

Left: Some legends say the travellers arrived in early summer, in time to see the pohutukawa flowering.

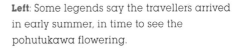

Key points about Maori arrivals

- Maori came to Aotearoa from eastern Polynesia.
- Their voyages were deliberate and carefully planned.
- They were expert sailors.
- They arrived in about AD 1350.
- They brought with them the kumara, the kiore and the dog.

Recently bones from the kiore (the rat that could only have got here with humans) have been found that are said to be 2000 years old. Perhaps there were some very early human arrivals who died out and left no other evidence.

We cannot prove that Maori were here before AD 1400, and we cannot prove that they were not. An estimated date of AD 1350 agrees with some of the Maori traditions and is not too far from what the archaeologists think.

Below: This map of the Pacific shows the huge distance that needed to be covered to reach New Zealand.

Above: Some kiore bones found recently are thought to be 2000 years old.

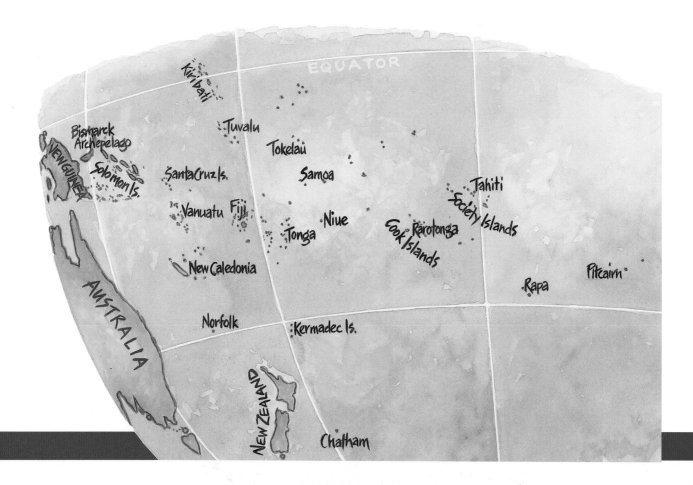

Maori settlement

Aotearoa's first settlers found a very different place from the warm, low-lying atolls and small Pacific islands they had left. Aotearoa must have seemed vast, with high mountains and a cooler climate. Some of the tropical plants quickly died out. The kumara could grow only in the warmer areas. But the sea teemed with life and there were plenty of birds.

POUNAMU

In the south were deposits of pounamu, the hard but decorative greenstone, which was valuable for trade. Off the coast of Tauranga, on Tuhua (Mayor Island), there were great deposits of obsidian. This black volcanic stone has very sharp edges and was useful for cutting and shaping tools.

The oldest tools, weapons, fish hooks and decorative objects are very like those made in eastern Polynesia. A pearl shell used to make a trolling lure shank found in Tairua, in the Coromandel, could only have come from eastern Polynesia.

Right: Pounamu was used to make decorative items like this tiki.

HUNTING

The first arrivals hunted seals, dolphins and moa. They made big catches of snapper, trevally and kahawai. They lived in groups of several small families, often making seasonal camps where the hunting was good.

They killed moa in large numbers. Sometimes they butchered hundreds in one

Below: High snowy mountains like Aoraki (Mt Cook), New Zealand's highest mountain, were new to people arriving from the Pacific.

Above: Kumara storage pits meant that kumara were protected over winter. This is a post-European kumara storage pit.

spot over a short period of time. Kiore and kuri (Polynesian dogs) ate moa eggs. When forests burned down, the surviving moa lost their habitat. Soon the moa was wiped out, probably 60 to 120 years after the first humans arrived. Some smaller species may have hung on. Some early European settlers on the west coast of the South Island reported seeing or hearing a large bird, too big for a kiwi, with a rattle-like call. It might have been the last moa.

FOOD SHORTAGES

In the 15th century the climate became rather cooler. There was a shortage of food. There were no more snapper off the South Island. In the north the average size of snapper was much smaller.

Kumara and bracken became the main foods. People burnt off bush so that bracken would grow. Skeletons from this period have teeth worn down by the harsh diet. There were

Below: Early Maori fished for kahawai (pictured), snapper and trevally.

Above: Moa were hunted for food. This picture shows what early moa-hunting villages were thought to have looked like.

fewer people. They died young, often in their twenties.

When the climate improved people cleared fertile garden land. Rua (underground pits) lined with bracken protected the tubers of kumara over winter so that they were ready for spring planting. The population increased again.

Left: Fish hooks like this pounamu one were decorative as well as useful.

When the first Europeans arrived in the 17th century they saw strong fortifications and defence sites. Competition for fertile garden land and good fishing places made Maori society unsettled and warlike.

MAORI SOCIETY

The whanau (extended family of three generations) was headed by kaumatua (male elder) and kuia (female elder). The whanau lived in the papakainga (village) and, except for defence, looked after itself. Beliefs about mana (status), utu (payback for injury or insult) and tapu (sacred matters) formed the rules for living. Sickness, death and urupa (cemeteries) could be tapu because Maori thought they were unclean.

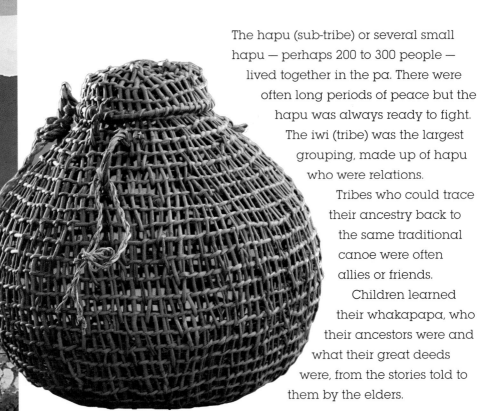

The hapu (sub-tribe) or several small hapu — perhaps 200 to 300 people — lived together in the pa. There were often long periods of peace but the hapu was always ready to fight. The iwi (tribe) was the largest grouping, made up of hapu who were relations.

Tribes who could trace their ancestry back to the same traditional canoe were often allies or friends.

Children learned their whakapapa, who their ancestors were and what their great deeds were, from the stories told to them by the elders.

Above: Woven fish traps like this korotete could be set and left to catch fish.

Below: As competition for land and food increased, Maori began to fortify their villages against attack. This village is at Ohinemutu on Lake Rotorua.

Key points about Maori settlement

- Early Maori settlers lived by hunting moa, fishing and growing kumara.
- When the climate went through a cold patch it was hard to find enough to eat.
- They competed fiercely for good fishing areas and good gardens.

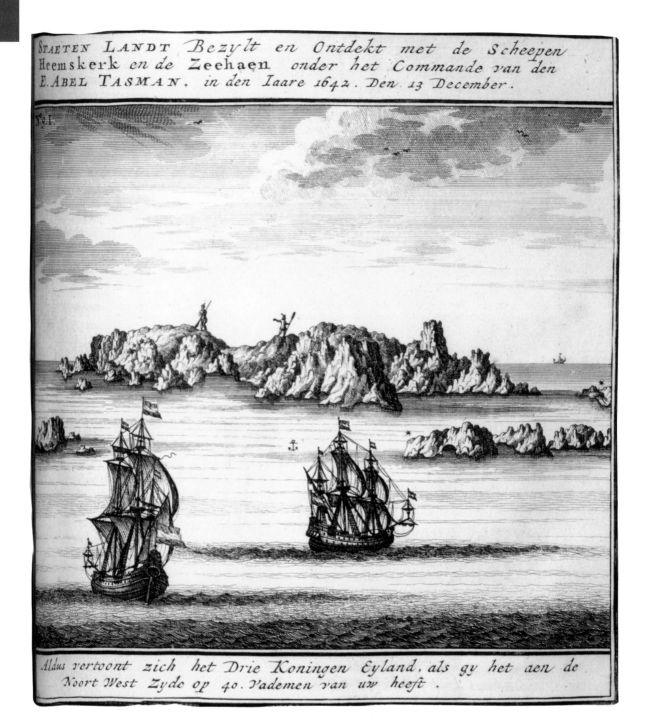

Staeten Landt Bezylt en Ontdekt met de Scheepen Heemskerk en de Zeehaen onder het Commande van den E. Abel Tasman, in den Iaare 1642. Den 13 December.

Aldus vertoont zich het Drie Koningen Eyland, als gy het aen de Noort West Zyde op 40. Vademen van uw heeft.

European explorers

ABEL TASMAN

Abel Tasman was a Dutch sea captain. The Dutch had a big trading empire in south-east Asia. They were keen to find new places to trade.

In 1642 Abel Tasman was told to sail east to discover what lay beyond Australia. He was given two ships, a fighting ship called the *Heemskerck* and a smaller, faster ship called the *Zeehaen*.

Above: The sea was quite rough so the ships sheltered in a protected bay, now called Tasman Bay.

After seven days of sailing from Tasmania they saw the west coast of the South Island. The sea was quite rough so the ships sheltered in a bay at the top of the island. They saw smoke from fires on the shore. Tasman hoped to make friends, and see if the people wanted to trade. His ships also needed fresh water.

Above: The Dutch sea captain, Abel Tasman.

> ### Key points about Abel Tasman
> - He was the first man from Europe to visit New Zealand and go back and tell the story. He drew charts of part of the coast.
> - He called the new land New Zealand after an area in Holland.
> - He told people in Europe that the Maori were fierce, tough and dangerous. This was one reason that it was 126 years before the next European visitors.

He sent a boat ashore. But he could not understand the Maori language and the Maori didn't understand Dutch. The boat did not even reach the shore. Four men were killed.

Tasman took fright, pulled up his anchors and sailed north. He called the bay Murderers' Bay. Today we call it Golden Bay.

Earlier arrivals?

William Colenso found part of a bell with Tamil writing on it in 1836. Part of an old Spanish helmet was dredged up out of Wellington Harbour. No one knows how it got there. Ancient shipwrecks have been reported on the northern west coast of New Zealand. Some people say these show there were other people who explored New Zealand first. But there is no hard evidence of anyone before Tasman.

CAPTAIN COOK

James Cook was born in 1728 in Cleveland, Yorkshire, in north-east England. His father was a farm worker and James did farm chores too. When his father became the foreman on a farm, James was able to go to school. He was good at mathematics. At age 12 he began work as a shop assistant in a haberdashery and grocery shop in a small fishing village. Before long he was working on the ships that sailed out of the town and learning as much about seamanship as he could.

Career

Cook served an apprenticeship on small coastal ships collecting and delivering coal. He was eager to study and learn. He was working his way up to be captain. Suddenly in 1755 he joined the Royal Navy instead, as an able seaman. His first posting was on the HMS *Eagle*. He rose quickly through the ranks. By the age of 28 he had passed his master's examination. At 39 he was a first lieutenant, at 42 a commander, at 46 a post captain. This was very unusual for someone who started as a farm boy. The officers who wrote reports on him often used the word 'genius'.

Below: Once a coal ship, the *Endeavour* proved to be ideal for exploring. This drawing was done by a crew member on the ship when it came to New Zealand.

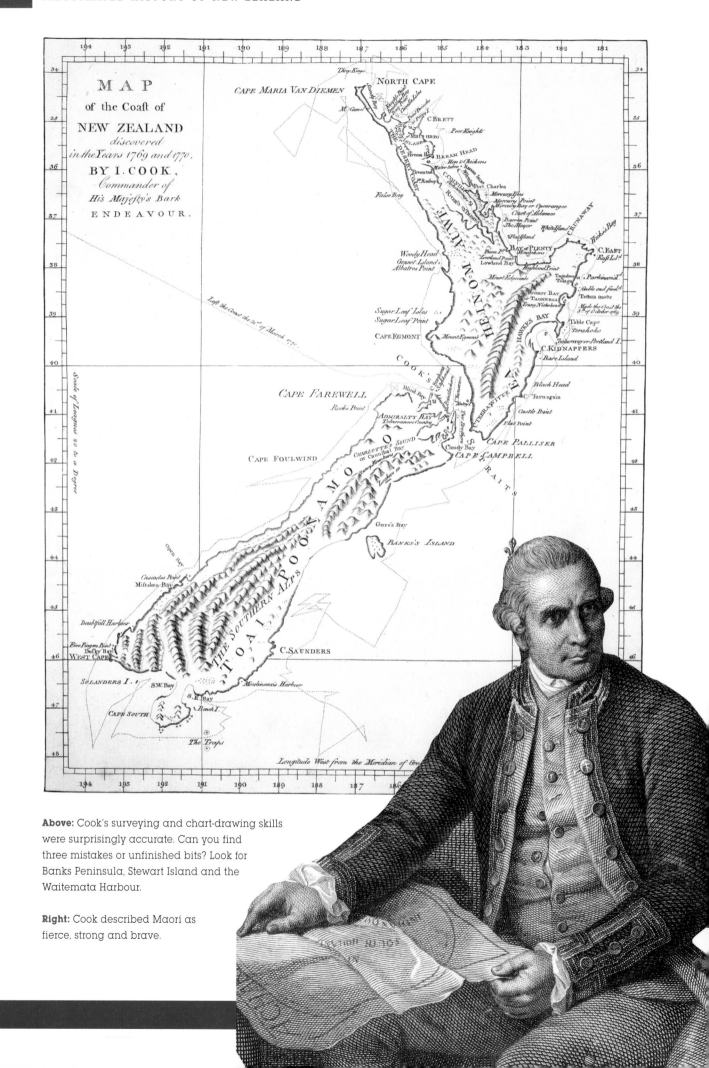

Above: Cook's surveying and chart-drawing skills were surprisingly accurate. Can you find three mistakes or unfinished bits? Look for Banks Peninsula, Stewart Island and the Waitemata Harbour.

Right: Cook described Māori as fierce, strong and brave.

Above: Cook and his men kept accurate records of Maori life. Sydney Parkinson drew this war canoe.

Right: The Maori were fierce but ready to learn new things.

Skills

When he was in the Royal Navy, fighting in the Seven Years War against the French in North America, he learned navigation, surveying and astronomy. When he was transferred to HMS *Pembroke* he met Samuel Holland, an army surveyor-engineer who taught him to survey and to draw charts. He made many charts of the St Lawrence River as far as Quebec and after the war spent several summers surveying and charting Newfoundland. In 1767 he wrote a paper about a solar eclipse for the Royal Society. The Royal Society decided he was just the man to take charge of their 1768 expedition to the South Seas.

Three voyages

1768–71: On the first voyage HMS *Endeavour* set sail from Plymouth, England, on Friday 26 August 1768. The plan was to take scientists to Tahiti to observe the transit of Venus across the sun on 3 June 1769. Then Cook was to look for the mythical 'Great Southern Continent', *Terra Australis Incognita*. The voyage circum-navigated the world and took three years. On this expedition he accurately charted both islands of New Zealand and more than 3000 kilometres of the Australian eastern coastline.

1772–75: The second voyage had two ships, HMS *Resolution* and HMS *Adventure*. They were to explore the South Pacific, using Queen Charlotte Sound in New Zealand and Tahiti as places for rest and repairs. As a result of this very successful expedition Cook was elected a Fellow of the Royal Society — a great honour for a farm boy.

1776–79: The third voyage also had two ships, HMS *Resolution* and HMS *Discovery*. They were to find a route to the Pacific around the top of Canada, and return a Tahitian called Omai to his homeland. Cook was 47, often in poor health, tired, and made more mistakes. In Hawaii he was killed. The expedition carried on and explored and charted a large section of the North American coast. It returned to England in 1779 without its leader.

Leadership

Cook's crew respected him. Only very occasionally did he joke and relax with them.

Above: Captain Cook was killed in a fight in the Sandwich Islands (Hawaii).

As usual in those times, discipline on board ship was strict and harsh. But Cook tried hard to look after his men and to keep them healthy. He was especially careful about diet. Special provisions like sauerkraut (salted and fermented cabbage) and carrot marmalade were taken. Cook insisted that the crew gather and eat lots of fresh greens. No one died of scurvy on Cook's ships though it was a killer disease for seamen on long voyages.

What Cook thought of New Zealand

He thought it was a good, rich land. Cook described the Maori as fierce, strong and brave. He tried hard to convince them that he came in peace and was very upset when blood was shed. There was some suspicion and violence but more friendship, trading and exchange of gifts.

What Maori thought of Captain Cook

- They were not scared of his strange new ship.
- They wanted to trade, especially to get the amazing iron goods like nails and axes. But when the ships stayed too long in one bay, there were too many extra mouths to feed, the food ran out and the ships were not welcome any more.

Brewing beer

Cook was the first man to make beer in New Zealand. He thought it would help to fight against scurvy. He boiled rimu bark and leaves for four hours, took out the branches, added molasses and some of his own beer. After a few days it was ready.

Key points about Captain Cook

- He was a bold explorer.
- He was a skilful and accurate map and chart maker.
- He rose from farm boy to famous explorer by hard work.
- He found out new facts about new lands and recorded them accurately.
- He cared about his crew and about keeping them healthy.
- He tried hard to be fair to native peoples and worried when his crew hurt them.

FRENCH EXPLORERS

The French had good maps and charts. Their explorers were very interested in New Zealand.

Jean Francois Marie de Surville

De Surville's ship, the *St Jean Baptiste*, crossed tracks with Cook's ship on 16 December 1769 in the north of New Zealand but neither ship saw the other. De Surville's men were dying of scurvy. Scurvy comes from not having enough vitamin C. On long sea voyages with no fresh green vegetables or fruit, men became very sick and often died. De Surville anchored in Doubtless Bay, close to a big Maori settlement. He threw the dead men into the harbour, where the local Maori did their fishing. After a boat went missing de Surville kidnapped one of the Maori who had helped him. De Surville sailed away with Te Ranginui, even though he begged not to be taken. Te Ranginui later died of scurvy. Maori were horrified by the way these newcomers behaved.

Marc Joseph Marion du Fresne

Three years later Marion du Fresne visited the Bay of Islands. His two ships, *Mascarin* and *Marquis de Castries*, were also badly affected by scurvy. The dying men, with their sores oozing pus, were an upsetting sight for Maori. Marion du Fresne stayed too long — for nearly two months — and 15 of his crew were killed. The survivors took revenge, burning villages and killing 300 Maori.

Above: The French commander Jules Sébastien César Dumont d'Urville explored the coast in his ship the *Astrolabe* — here sailing through French Pass in 1827.

How Maori saw the explorers

- New trade goods like cloth, axes and nails were very popular.
- The guns were very scary. They wanted guns too.
- The new people were dangerous, they sometimes stayed too long and ate all the food.

Key points about early European explorers

- They were interested mostly in trade.
- They could not speak or understand Maori and did not understand Maori rules like tapu.
- Sometimes misunderstandings ended in death.
- They brought new trade goods but diseases as well.

Below: Death of Marion du Fresne at the Bay of Islands, New Zealand, 12 June 1772.

Sealing, whaling, timber and trade

Sealers and whalers stayed a short time in New Zealand. They did not want to live here. They wanted to make money from taking natural resources and selling the products to people in Europe, China and America. A few got to like it, and stayed on to live with Maori women and have families. They needed to get protection from a Maori tribe to trade or develop a farm.

Above: A fur seal.

SEALING

Seals were plentiful and easy to kill. Sealers could get 14,000 first-class skins in one season. Seal skins made very fashionable hats and sold in China, America and England.

Sealers were rough, tough men. Some were escaped convicts. The leaders were violent and sometimes flogged their men. They set up temporary camps close to the shore and lived there for months or years. Most camps were on the southern coast of the South Island or on the offshore islands.

But by 1810 the fashion changed and anyway seals were not so plentiful.

WHALING

Before electricity, candles were too expensive for many people. Whale-oil lamps were smelly but cheap. The oil was used for lubrication too. From a waxy substance in the spout of the sperm whale, high-quality candles, ointments and cosmetics were made. Perfumes were made from the ambergris found in the whales' intestines.

Deep-sea whaling

Deep-sea whalers hunted the sperm whale (cachalot). They needed food, fresh water and time on shore between trips. The deep-sea whaling ships found that Kororareka (now Russell) in the Bay of Islands was an ideal sheltered anchorage with food, water and entertainment. Kororareka became a rough

Below: A sealers' camp. The sealers are preparing a meal of fish and seabirds. The birds that they are eating are probably muttonbirds.

Stewart del.

Above: Kororareka was a sheltered anchorage but when the whalers were in, it was a wild town.

whaling town with pubs, lots of heavy drinking, swearing and fighting. Some Maori served on whaling ships as crew.

Bay whaling

After 1820 bay whaling developed. This was shore-based whaling, using small, sturdy whale boats to hunt the black or right whale for oil and bone. Whalebone was used for

Above: Whaling was a dangerous way to earn a living.

women's corsets, for umbrella ribs and upholstery packing. The whaling season was May to October. Whaling stations were little villages with small children, Maori wives, houses and small farms. When new settlers arrived in Otago, whalers like Johnny Jones supplied them with food. Dicky Barrett, a Tory Channel whaler, helped new settlers in the Wellington area. Barrett's Reef in Wellington Harbour is named after him.

By the 1850s whaling had disappeared. Demand for the products had changed and there were fewer whales.

Below: Huge pots were used to boil up whale meat to extract whale oil.

TIMBER

New Zealand forests produced wonderful timber. The long, straight trunks of the kauri and rimu were ideal for masts and booms on sailing ships. The British Royal Navy was very keen on New Zealand spars of kauri and rimu. Maori preferred totara for canoes.

Forests grew close to the coast in North Auckland (Hokianga Harbour especially) and the Coromandel region. With trees growing close to sheltered, deep water, the logs could be loaded straight onto waiting ships. Later trees had to be taken from further inland. Saw mills were set up and the timber industry became an important way for people to earn a living.

Above: A house and timber yard at Kohukohu in the Hokianga Harbour. The ship in the picture is loading kauri for export.

Left: Maori preferred totara to kauri for canoes. After special prayers to Tane the god of the forest, the totara was felled. The interior was carefully burnt and carved out. Often several trees were used to build the huge war canoes.

Tane Mahuta

- Tane Mahuta is the tallest kauri in New Zealand.
- It is thought to be 2100 years old.
- Its scientific name is *Agathis Australis*.
- You can visit Tane Mahuta in the Waipoua State Forest in Northland.
- It is 51.54 metres tall.

TRADE

The first European traders wanted food and water for their whaling ships. They would barter European goods for potatoes and pork. This trading suited both sides and meant they needed to get on well together. Maori wanted clothes, nails and axes, but above all they were very keen on getting muskets. The price of muskets kept going up.

Flax trading

Flax fibre of very good quality was produced from New Zealand flax. It was made into ropes and cords. They prepared the fibre by scraping the fleshy part of the flax with a sharp mussel shell. Maori women did the work. Fibre got a good price but took a long time to produce. Using a system of barter instead of money, traders swapped muskets (light guns) for cargoes of flax. One tonne of fibre would be swapped for one or two muskets. However after 1831 it was easier to use Manila fibre from the Philippines.

Below: Flax cutting.

Below right: Men in a paddock with rows of drying flax fibre.

Hongi Hika

Traders and missionaries needed the protection of a powerful chief. In the north they were protected by Hongi Hika, chief of the very strong Ngapuhi. In 1820 Hongi Hika was taken to England by the missionary Thomas Kendall. He helped scholars put together a Maori dictionary. He was very popular in England and was even presented to the King. The King gave him a suit of armour. Hongi Hika got lots of other presents too. But before he came back to New Zealand he sold all his presents and bought 300 muskets. He kept the suit of armour.

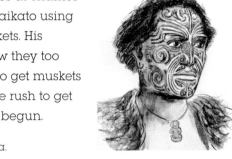

Once he was home again he attacked his old Maori enemies at Thames and in the Waikato using his new muskets. His enemies knew they too would have to get muskets to survive. The rush to get muskets had begun.

Right: Hongi Hika.

Key points about early trade

- Traders needed the protection of a Maori chief.
- Whalers and sealers were mostly just visiting.
- Maori and the traders, whalers and sealers did not want to fight each other. They all needed peace to trade.

Missionaries and musket wars

Samuel Marsden arrived from Sydney in 1814 to set up a Church of England mission station with a schoolmaster, a carpenter and a ropemaker.

PROTECTION OF A CHIEF

The mission was established in the Bay of Islands under the protection of Hongi Hika. The fierce warrior chief of Ngapuhi wanted the mission because it would bring trade and perhaps muskets, but he refused to be a Christian. He said it was not a good religion for a warrior. The mission made no converts until 1825.

MORE MISSIONS

Later Marsden's mission moved to Kerikeri. Another big Anglican mission was established at Waimate where Bishop Selwyn was based. The farm grew wheat and other crops.

Above: Samuel Marsden arrived from Sydney in 1814.

Methodists set up the Wesleyan mission at Mangungu, on the Hokianga Harbour. Bishop Pompallier came to New Zealand in 1838 to be the leader of the Catholic church and to encourage Maori to become Christian.

Below: A meeting between missionaries and Maori at Kaitaia.

Above: The English missionary establishment at Kerikeri in 1824.

A mission station usually had a house for the missionary's family, a chapel for worship, and a schoolroom. Sometimes there were sleeping quarters for children or adults being trained as teachers. The mission farm grew most of the food.

Left: Bishop Jean-Baptiste François Pompallier.

Below: William Colenso set up a small press to print bibles in Maori.

Above: Kororareka, now known as Russell, was the major settlement in New Zealand in 1838.

Key points about missionaries

- There were never many missionaries at one time. Most areas were not affected by them.
- They did not live with Maori as traders did, but set up little islands of Pakeha culture.
- Maori were very keen to learn to read the Bible. Printer William Colenso could barely keep up with demand.
- Missionaries despised traders for trading in muskets but they too found it very hard to resist Maori demands to sell them muskets or repair them.
- Some of the missionaries, like Henry Williams, managed to get vast areas of land for their families.
- Missionaries worried about protecting the Maori from the rough, hard-drinking whalers, sealers and traders, especially the ones at Kororareka.

Above: A musket was an early type of gun.

THE MUSKET WARS

Ngapuhi and their chief Hongi Hika were the first to get muskets. They raided a wide area from the Waikato to Te Whanganui-a-Tara (Wellington). The Waikato tribes then got muskets and raided their neighbours, squeezing out the small Ngati Toa tribe from Kawhia. Their leader, Te Rauparaha, led his people south, first to Taranaki and then to the Otaki area, Kapiti Island and the northern part of the South Island. Many Maori died in these Musket Wars of the 1820s and 1830s. Tribes were pushed off land they had lived on for many years. Who owned which part of the land became very muddled.

Below: The wounded chief Hongi Hika, surrounded by his family at Kororareka in November 1827.

Disease

Many Maori also died from diseases brought by the Pakeha. Because the Polynesians had been moving across the Pacific in small numbers for thousands of years, diseases like influenza, measles and chicken pox had died out. When they mixed with the Pakeha — trading, working, marrying or sleeping with them — diseases which just made the Pakeha a bit sick made the Maori so sick that many of them died. We don't know how many died but we do know that some places were devastated. In Auckland in the 1820s, for example, the great pa of Mangawhau was deserted because so many Ngati Whatua died of disease. They believed evil spirits had taken over the pa.

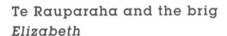

Above: Te Rauparaha.

Above: The *Tory* arrives in Wellington in 1839 to survey a possible place to settle.

Te Rauparaha and the brig *Elizabeth*

In 1830 Te Rauparaha got Captain John Stewart of the brig *Elizabeth* to take a raiding party of 100 warriors to Akaroa. There he surprised his old enemies Ngai Tahu and killed them. This massacre horrified the authorities but they were even more horrified that Captain Stewart had helped Te Rauparaha. Captain Stewart disappeared before he could be punished. The authorities in New South Wales who were keeping an eye on things in New Zealand said New Zealand was a place without law and no one was safe.

Settlers on their way

And there was another worry. Settlers from Britain were making plans to come to the Wellington area and make their own rules. The British government was very concerned. Would the settlers treat Maori properly? Would they pay a fair price for the land? Would Maori like Te Rauparaha use the Pakeha to carry out more revenge on other tribes?

What could be done?

The British government appointed a British Resident for New Zealand in 1833. He was James Busby. His job was to bring law and order to the country. But he did not have enough power. He tried to set up a Northern Confederation of Chiefs, with their own flag, but the violence and disorder continued. Maori called him 'the man-o'-war without guns'.

There was a strange Frenchman, Baron Charles de Thierry, who said he was going to be the Sovereign Chief of New Zealand. No one took much notice of him but Busby was rather worried about him.

Below: James Busby suggested that a New Zealand flag would encourage Maori chiefs to work together. Rev. Henry Williams designed three flags and on 20 March 1834, 25 chiefs from the Far North got together and chose this flag. It became known as the flag of the United Tribes of New Zealand.

Treaty of Waitangi

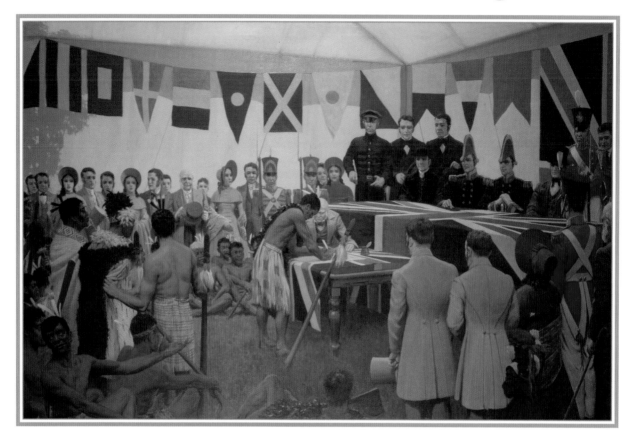

Above: A reconstruction of the signing of the Treaty of Waitangi.

On 5 February 1840 a large group of people met together at Waitangi in the Bay of Islands.

From early on, canoes had been seen gliding across the bay to the lawn outside Mr Busby's house on a headland above the water. Ships were at anchor showing their different national flags. The weather was fine and clear. Boats with Pakeha settlers and people who lived in the Bay of Islands landed at the shore. On the lawn was a large tent with an English Union Jack flying proudly. About 40 Maori chiefs were waiting, some dressed in fine cloaks or dogskin mats of black and white stripes. Others were dressed in European clothes. Some wore new woollen cloaks of crimson, blue, brown or plaid.

CAPTAIN HOBSON

In the tent sat an important British naval officer dressed in his naval uniform, all gold stripes and brass buttons. His name was Captain William Hobson. He had been sent by the British government. He had been given clear instructions. He was to call together the Maori chiefs and persuade them that Great Britain should take over the job of governing the northern part of New Zealand. Only the government would be able to buy land from Maori. In return Maori would get to keep their lands and property, and they would have the rights and privileges of British subjects. Then he should claim the South Island as British because Captain Cook, from Britain, had been the first to land there.

HENRY WILLIAMS

Hobson had prepared a document listing what the chiefs would get to keep and what they would have to give up. One of the missionaries, Reverend Henry Williams, had quickly translated the document into Maori the night before. And now Henry Williams (dressed in sober black with Harry Potter glasses) translated into Maori as Hobson explained the Treaty to all the chiefs gathered there.

Henry Williams invented some new words to put the ideas into Maori. For example he used the word kawanatanga to describe the British government ruling over New Zealand. Some think a better word might have been mana. The English word is sovereignty. Henry Williams was not feeling too comfortable because he had bought 4500 hectares very cheaply from the Maori and was a bit worried about whether he would be allowed to keep all of it. But he was keen to persuade the chiefs to sign.

BISHOP POMPALLIER

Bishop Pompallier was there, dressed in dark purple robes with a glistening gold chain and crucifix. He asked if people would be allowed to worship their own god or gods as they wanted. He was worried that the British might be anti-Catholic because they were mostly Anglican, that is Protestant. Yes, said Hobson, everyone would be free to worship how they liked.

THE CHIEFS

The day was spent in speeches. Some Maori chiefs spoke against signing the Treaty. Some told the white men to go away, and take their foreign goods with them. Others like Tamati Waka Nene said it was too late for that. They should have sent the traders home a generation ago. He called on Hobson to stay, to help the Maori keep their lands and their customs.

Above: Tamati Waka Nene.

One chief complained that a Pakeha had sworn at him. Would that be how things went on? Another asked how the governor would stop the Pakeha traders lying, and stealing from the Maori. Hobson said the new government would protect their lands. 'Well,' said one Maori chief, 'the missionaries have got most of mine!'

THE SIGNING

The next day, 6 February 1840, they all met again. At first no one would sign. Then Busby called out each Maori chief by name. The missionary printer Colenso, who spoke Maori well, interrupted. He did not think that the chiefs could really understand the Treaty. But Hobson brushed him aside.

Most of the chiefs signed, even those who

James Busby

James Busby was the British Resident in New Zealand in 1840. The house we now know as the Treaty House at Waitangi was built by Busby. It is only a small two-bedroom house but he lived there with his wife and six children.

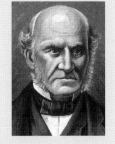

had spoken against the Treaty the day before. They got a present of tobacco.

Why did the chiefs sign?

Perhaps they were worried about other chiefs or tribes getting ahead of them. Anyway, in February 1840 there were 10 times as many Maori as Pakeha in New Zealand. Who could predict that one day the Pakeha would be so many that the Maori would be outnumbered?

Around the country

Hobson made copies of the Treaty. He took them around the country. Many chiefs signed. Some signed the English copy, some signed the Maori copy. Some chiefs did not sign. It took several months to hold meetings and collect signatures.

Meanwhile a group of new settlers from England had landed at Port Nicholson

Above: When Wellington was first built it was called Port Nicholson. This is what it looked like in 1840 when the Treaty of Waitangi was signed.

(Wellington) and were making their own laws. To stop this, Hobson issued a proclamation on 21 May 1840, signed by Queen Victoria, which declared that all of New Zealand was ruled by Great Britain.

Key points about the Treaty

- Maori chiefs were to hand over their power to Queen Victoria.
- In return they were to have the rights and privileges of British subjects.
- Their lands and possessions were guaranteed.
- They were to sell land only to the government.
- Different versions of the Treaty were signed in different places.
- We have been arguing ever since about what the Treaty really means.

Left: On 17 February 1840 Maori gathered on the verandah at Waimate mission to sign the treaty.

Left: Rangi Topeora, the sister of Te Rangihaeata, was one of the few women to sign the Treaty of Waitangi.

Pioneer settlers

Most new settlers came from England, Scotland, Wales and Ireland. Over there life for most people was hard and the rich were far above them.

They had little chance of bettering themselves, of ever buying their own land or sending their children to university, or setting up a business. Many left to give their children a better chance in life.

VOYAGE OUT

It was very sad saying goodbye to families they would probably never see again, knowing that any news from home would be months old. The voyage to New Zealand took four months, or more if the weather was bad. The leaky ships were crowded and uncomfortable. Fresh food and water were scarce. If there was illness it would spread rapidly through the ship. Lots of small children died. With no fresh water for washing, it was uncomfortable going through the tropics. Still, they were going to a new land, a new life with great hopes for the future.

Passengers in steerage (the lowest class of travel) were very crowded.

Below left: Conditions onboard emigrant ships were cramped and uncomfortable.

Below: Captain Cargill, the leader of the Otago settlement.

DINNER ON BOARD THE FIRST EMIGRANT SHIP FOR NEW ZEALAND.

Below: **Below:** Local Taranaki Maori help Rev. Waterhouse and other missionaries to come ashore from their ship.

Above: Edward Gibbon Wakefield was one of the main men behind the New Zealand Company.

Sheep farming turned out to be a better option for many. And there just weren't enough good people wanting to come. But though the schemes didn't quite turn out as Wakefield hoped, they did bring lots of people to New Zealand.

OTHER KINDS OF SETTLEMENT

Wakefield didn't organise all the settlement. There were later groups like the Nova Scotians who went to Waipu, the Scandinavians to Dannevirke and Norsewood, the Bohemians to Puhoi, and the Germans to Nelson. Still others

WAKEFIELD'S SETTLEMENT SCHEME

Some settlers came in organised schemes like the New Zealand Company schemes in Wellington, Nelson, New Plymouth, Canterbury and Otago. This was the idea of Edward Gibbon Wakefield, who was a bit of a crook. He had served time in jail in England for abducting an heiress.

His plan was to select immigrants carefully so only hard-working, good people came. He wanted everyone to live on little farms growing crops. This did not always work out.

Right: The *Ellen Lewis* brought settlers from Nova Scotia in Canada to Waipu in Northland in 1860.

came on their own or in small groups. They went to places like Auckland and Russell. Later, when gold was discovered, they rushed in big numbers to parts of Otago, the west coast of the South Island and Thames.

What to bring

There were almost no shops or factories in New Zealand so people knew they had to bring lots of stuff with them. There was a good chance of buying food from Maori farms or from the whaler Johnny Jones in Otago, but they needed the tools to grow their own food as quickly as possible. Farm tools were a must, as well as clothes, pots and pans. Medicines too, and books — no wonder the ships were loaded down with baggage. Men were advised to give themselves an extra week to choose a good wife to bring with them! Having a wife was very important, because starting off a farm in the wilderness of New Zealand was going to be very difficult if you did not have a working partner.

Above left: Auckland as it looked on 1 October 1840.

Above: William Deans and his brother lived on a farm at Riccarton.

Somewhere to live

The first job was to build a shelter from raupo, or a more permanent house from wood. Luckily there was plenty of wood for building. In the south, houses were often made from cob (a mixture of earth, gravel and turf). It took some settlers a while to learn they had to build houses facing north to make the most of the sunshine, rather than south as in the northern hemisphere.

Clearing land

The next job was to clear the land. In bush-covered country this was a huge job. Many hectares of forest were burnt off to speed up the process. Grass or crops were planted between the stumps of giant trees. Even getting rid of the stumps later involved lots of work. In the south, where Maori had already burnt off the bush, it was easier. Soon farmers were bringing flocks of sheep into the Wairarapa and the Canterbury Plains.

Left: No wonder that the ships carried a lot of baggage.

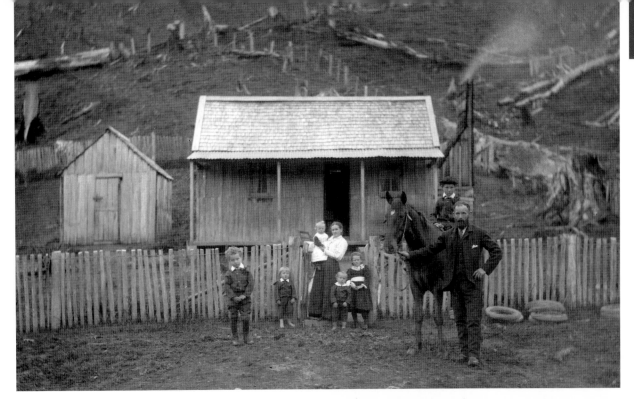

Above: A Taranaki family with a new house. The tree stumps in the background show that the land is still being cleared.

What the women did

Keeping the family fed, clothed and healthy was the woman's full-time job. Cooking was often on an open fire, water had to be fetched from the stream, bread had to be baked at home. Sometimes women made butter to sell in nearby settlements. Families were often large, but many children died young of whooping cough, typhoid or diarrhoea.

What the men did

Men cleared the land and looked after the livestock. Accidents when they were cutting down trees were very common.

What the children did

Children were expected to work hard, helping on the farm and with household tasks. They were much more independent and resourceful than their English cousins. They rode horses and could be trusted with serious jobs. It was their job to keep up the wood supply for cooking. They washed clothes, helped Dad clear stumps off the land, and looked after the little kids. They did not go to school regularly until much later. They mostly went barefoot because shoes had to be imported and were expensive.

Above: This is how the inside of a settler's hut might have looked.

Key points about pioneer settlers

- Within six years of the signing of the Treaty of Waitangi there were 9000 new settlers.
- Maori farmers sold them food but were horrified by the numbers. Were these people taking over?
- Many settlers were from towns or cities and found country living difficult.
- There were few roads. To get anywhere you went by sea. There were many shipwrecks and drownings.
- Settlers quickly learned about their new land, for example, how to make tea from manuka leaves, and not to eat the poisonous berries of the tutu bush.

Gold

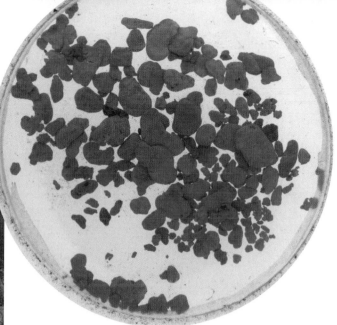

Above: Gold dust and nuggets.

Left: Gold miners built temporary houses. The three men on the right are Chinese miners.

GABRIEL'S GULLY

The Otago provincial council knew there was gold in its region. There had been small finds. In 1861 it offered £500 (in 2003 this would be worth $60,000) for anyone who found gold.

An Australian man called Gabriel Read went prospecting in the Tuapeka area, near Lawrence. He took a tent, a spade, a tin dish, a blanket, a butcher's knife and a week's food. He found 7 ounces (200 grams) of gold. He reported it to the Superintendent of Otago. Within a few weeks there were 11,000 men in a tent city at Gabriel's Gully, chasing the dream of getting rich from gold. It was called 'gold fever'. Miners had to have a licence called a 'miner's right' to dig or pan for gold.

Below: A mail coach, with its many passengers, about to leave the township of Dunstan (now known as Clyde) for Roxburgh, in the 1880s. The Dunstan Hotel is alongside, and the Hartley Arms Hotel is also just visible.

Above: In Thames, tramways like the one in this picture were used to transport gold. This is the Una claim which was worked from 1868 until 1930. Over this time it produced 30,000 ounces of gold.

DIFFERENT TYPES OF GOLD MINING

The first gold found was alluvial, which means it was found in river beds. It was gold washed out of a seam in the rock by the rivers. When the easy alluvial gold had been found, shafts had to be dug, sluices and even dredges used on the deeper rivers. This needed more money, and companies were formed to work the gold fields.

In Thames there was little alluvial gold. Expensive machinery was needed to work the quartz reefs. Stampers were needed to crush the ore (gold-bearing rock). Gold was extracted from the ore by a chemical process.

Below: Big gold dredges, like this one near Cromwell, were used to mine gold commercially.

Above: The sluice at Switzer's claim. The fast-running water helped to separate the gold from the gravel.

DUNSTAN

In 1862 gold was discovered near the Clutha River and about 3000 men came to the diggings around Dunstan. A miner called William Fox came into the town for supplies. He sold a lot of gold but disappeared before people could see where he was going. Had he discovered a new field? At last the smoke from his cooking fire gave him away and the Arrow River rush was on. Later there were finds at Shotover and Naseby. There were finds of gold on the West Coast at Reefton and later in the North Island in Thames and Waihi.

Above: Chinese miners worked hard on difficult claims. Despite this they were often treated with suspicion by local people.

CHINESE MINERS

Some miners came all the way from China. They looked very different. The Emperor of China had made them wear their hair in long plaits. They carried their belongings in baskets slung over long poles. They wore large bamboo hats. Other miners often picked on them, and only allowed them to work in claims they thought were useless. But the Chinese were very hard workers and found gold even there. They lived simply in huts made from slabs of wood or stone. Many returned to China with their savings.

HOW THE BOOM AFFECTED TOWNS

Gold poured into Dunedin. People wanted supplies and entertainment. Dunedin, for a few years, became the largest and richest town in New Zealand. Big new buildings like banks were built. In 1870 Thames, with a population of 20,000, was bigger than Auckland.

Some towns flourished but when the gold

Key points about gold mining

- The miners were nearly all men. On the gold fields they made their own rough, tough rules for living.
- The gold rush lasted only a few years. By 1875 it was over.
- Gold is mined in New Zealand today, at Macraes Flat in Otago and in Waihi. Lots of huge machinery is needed.
- Gold mining brought lots of miners to New Zealand and some stayed on.
- The people who did best in the gold rushes were those who supplied the miners with goods.
- Because supplies came by sea, there were lots of shipwrecks on the wild West Coast.

Left: Carriage and passengers alongside Cobb & Co.

Below: The last Central Otago gold escort, changing horses at Roxburgh. The escort team is made up of policemen and Bank of New Zealand staff.

ran out they were deserted. Buildings fell into ruins or were shifted away. They became ghost towns. Lyall, Goldsborough and Stafford are good examples of abandoned towns which are still marked on maps. But today, where once there were churches, houses, shops and pubs, all you can find is an overgrown graveyard and some flat places where the houses used to be.

Right: The windy and dangerous road that leads into the Skippers Canyon didn't stop people from living in this remote and difficult place during the gold rush. A few people still live at Skippers today but they work in tourism and farming.

Conflict between the races

Maori and Pakeha needed peace. They traded with each other. Pakeha needed food, and Maori wanted European goods. There were lots of children who had both Maori and Pakeha blood.

MORE AND MORE PAKEHA

When Maori were in a majority they did not feel too threatened. But by 1858 there were equal numbers of Maori and Pakeha. And more Pakeha kept coming. Many of the new white settlers were arrogant and rude. They treated the Maori as dirty savages. Maori thought Pakeha were greedy and selfish. Even early on there were signs that there was trouble ahead.

Below: Te Rangihaeata.

WAIRAU AND TE RAUPARAHA

In Nelson in 1843 settlers wanted more land. They tried to push their way into the fertile Wairau plains by bullying the wily, tough old warrior Te Rauparaha and his fierce nephew Te Rangihaeata. Most of an armed posse of settlers who went to punish Te Rauparaha ended up dead. The Nelson settlers called this the Wairau Massacre. But the government would not support them. Later, however, Governor Grey got tired of Te Rauparaha harassing the Wellington settlement, caught him sleeping, took him prisoner, and kept him in jail without a trial.

NORTHERN WAR AND HONE HEKE

Ngapuhi chief Hone Heke was angry that the country's capital had been moved to Auckland. There were fewer whalers calling at Kororareka and less trade. He did not like not being able to sell land except to the government. Heke blamed the government and decided to attack the symbol of their rule. In 1844 and 1845 he cut down the flagstaff at Kororareka three times. He attacked the town.

Above: Hone Heke and his wife, Harriet.

GEORGE GREY

Governor George Grey, appointed by the British government in 1845, spoke Maori well. He wrote down Maori myths and legends. He made friends with the chiefs and gave money to mission schools and hospitals. His policy was to buy lots of land for Pakeha settlement. Where land was owned by the Pakeha, there was Pakeha law and authority. Where land was in Maori ownership, Maori law and authority ruled. But the settlers felt that there could only be one law and that was British law.

Below: Sir George Grey was Governor of New Zealand.

The small British force was defeated.

More British troops were sent to the north. At a battle at Ohaewai, Hone Heke and his ally Kawiti beat off the British force. However, at Ruapekapeka, Hone Heke and Kawiti were defeated. But neither was captured. Though the Maori were very good fighters they only had a part-time army. Their men had to go home to plant the kumara. The British army had full-time soldiers.

Above: The gnarled old warrior Te Wherowhero was the one man with the mana to be the new king.

THE MAORI KING MOVEMENT

In 1858 the Waikato tribes and their allies decided they should have their own king. They appointed a famous old warrior, Te Wherowhero, as King Potatau I. The word whero means red. His favourite cloak was a red blanket.

The King Movement became the first national Maori movement. It wanted to prevent all the land being sold. The movement stopped the Pakeha expansion into the rich, fertile land of the Waikato. The Pakeha were not happy. There was fierce fighting from 1858 until the mid-1860s between the Maori forces and the British army.

Taranaki War

The first fighting was in Taranaki. The New Plymouth settlers wanted more land. Ngati Awa did not want to sell them the fertile Waitara block. Governor Thomas Gore Browne wanted to buy the Waitara from a lesser chief. This made the main chief, Wiremu Kingi, very angry. But Gore Browne wanted to show him that the British were in charge.

When war began the King Movement sent Waikato warriors to help the Taranaki tribes. There were many fierce battles. The Maori army was outnumbered by the British army. But they fought so well that neither side clearly won and the war ended in an unhappy truce.

Pakeha settlers were very critical of the way

Below: The FitzRoy Pole marked the boundary between Ngati Awa land and the Taranaki settlers.

the war was fought. Governor Gore Browne was dismissed. The New Plymouth settlers were even worse off because the war had devastated Taranaki and the Waitara had to be given back to Ngati Awa.

PREPARATIONS FOR WAR

In 1861 Sir George Grey became governor again. He told the British government that the Waikato tribes were about to attack Auckland. He built roads south so that troops could move quickly. He had gunboats ready on the Waikato River. In 1863 he sent British troops across the Mangatawhiri Stream, the northern boundary of the King Movement's land.

The British army of 18,000 men was led by General Duncan Cameron. The Maori army had 1000 to 2000 men if they could get them together all at once. Because it was a part-time army the men kept having to go home to look after their gardens. Rewi Maniapoto, Wiremu Tamihana and Tikaokao were the most important Maori commanders.

Waikato War

At Meremere a Maori force managed to stop the gunboats going up the river for 14 weeks. But at Rangiriri, British forces overran the pa and captured 180 prisoners. Some of the Maori soldiers arrived after the battle was lost. Then the British force sneaked quietly past the great pa of Paterangi and sacked Rangiowhia, destroying a key Maori settlement in the richest farm area of the Waikato.

At a final battle at Orakau, Rewi Maniapoto made a brave but hopeless last stand. When the British commander asked him to surrender, he made the famous reply: 'E hoa, ka whawhai tonu akau kia koe ake ake ake.' ('Friend, I will go on fighting you for ever and ever.') Then the British commander said that the women and children should surrender. But a woman stood up and shouted out that if the men died then the women and children would die too. Many did die, but during the night many escaped into the bush and fled over the hills to Kawhia.

The British were not all that happy about the war. They had pushed the Waikato tribes south and taken lots of land but they had not had a great victory.

Below: Rewi Maniapoto.

Tauranga campaign

The British army decided to punish Ngai Te Rangi for supporting the Maori King. They thought that by attacking the King's allies at Tauranga they would show the power of the mighty British Empire and what good soldiers they were.

Above: Gustavus von Tempsky falling to his death after being shot at Te Ngutu o te Manu, Taranaki, on 7 September 1868.

A British force of 1700 men attacked Gate Pa. When they were sure no one could have survived their heavy bombardment, they stormed the pa. But the Ngai Te Rangi leader, Rawiri Puhirake, had built trenches underground where his force of 200 men had sheltered. Their withering fire killed the attacking British in large numbers. It was an unbelievable defeat for the British. A later victory at Te Ranga, when a patrol killed Rawiri Puhirake, made the British army look a bit better — but not much.

End of the Waikato War

Things did not look very good for the British army. The 200 Maori prisoners held on Kawau Island escaped. The British had conquered less than one-third of the land of the Waikato tribes. The King Movement was weakened but still there. True the Maori had lost some of their

Right: Members of the New Zealand Armed Constabulary in about 1879.

best farming land. Their trade was ruined. But General Cameron decided he had had enough. There was an uneasy truce.

LAND CONFISCATION

To pay for the war, and to punish the losers, land was taken away from the fighting tribes. Their land was to be sold to settlers and soldiers. About 1.4 million hectares was taken.

The loss of the land led to more fighting. Colonial troops, who were settler volunteers, did the fighting. They were helped by 'friendly' tribes. Sometimes these wars were like civil wars. Maori tribes were fighting their old enemies. Sometimes there were religious movements like Pai Marire, which stirred up fierce fighting. Some fighters like Titokowaru in Taranaki, or Te Kooti in Poverty Bay, made settlers despair. They thought the fighting would never end. In some areas like South Taranaki all the Maori villages were burnt to the ground.

Above: Te Ua Haumene, the founder and prophet of the Hauhau church.

Key points about conflict
- The wars were about who was to be in charge.
- Whichever side owned the land made the laws.
- Maori were great fighters but they had a part-time army.
- The British army and then the Colonial Volunteer Army had more men and could keep them fighting all year round.
- The wars ended in a muddled and unhappy way.
- Land confiscation hit Maori communities hard.

Political changes

From 1840 New Zealand was a British colony. A governor was appointed by the British government to administer the laws. The colonial secretary told him what to do. The new settlers soon wanted to have some say in how to run the country.

FEDERAL GOVERNMENT

In 1852 the British government set up a federal system of government in New Zealand. There were six provinces. There was a governor, still appointed by Britain, a legislative council of worthy men appointed for life by the governor (this was abolished in 1950) and a house of representatives elected by the people. At last the settlers were represented in government. Only those who owned property got to vote. Because they did not own their land as individuals, Maori did not have a vote.

Provinces

The provinces were Auckland, New Plymouth, Wellington, Nelson, Canterbury and Otago. Each one had an elected superintendent and an elected council to make laws for that province. Later some changes were made to the provinces. New Plymouth became Taranaki in 1858. New provinces were created. Hawke's Bay was added in 1858, Marlborough in 1859, Southland in 1861 and Westland in 1871.

The provinces had bad money troubles and were abolished in 1876. From then on New Zealand was administered as one country.

Above: New Zealand was a British colony and Victoria was Queen of New Zealand.

People power

Although the settlers were able to elect members to the House of Representatives from 1850, the governor still made the most important decisions. The settlers did not like this. They were pleased when after 1856 the governor was told by the British government to start handing over the real decision-making to the settlers.

By the 1890s the governor had to follow the advice of the elected ministers on all matters.

AN INDEPENDENT COUNTRY

In 1907 the British said New Zealand could be a dominion rather than a colony. This meant New Zealanders had more control over their own country. From 1931 New Zealand was completely independent from Britain, although this wasn't made official until 1947. After 1930 the governor-general was appointed on the advice of the New Zealand government.

Who could vote?

At first to vote you needed to be male, a British citizen, over 21 and to own some property. This meant that Maori, women and settlers who weren't British had no say in who went to parliament. In 1879 all adult males got the right to vote. If you owned property in another electorate besides the one you lived in you could vote there too. This was called plural voting. It ended in 1889. After that it was 'one man one vote'.

Maori representation

After 1867 Maori could vote for members of parliament, but only in four special Maori electorates. From 1879 they could choose whether to be on the general roll or the special Maori roll for electing members of parliament. After 1993 the Maori seats were increased and there are now seven. However a Maori can represent a general electorate. Sir James Carroll was the first to do so.

Above: This map shows the provinces.

Below: Some people didn't want New Zealand to change from a colony to a dominion. This cartoon by Trevor Lloyd shows the premier, Joseph Ward, trying to turn a kiwi into a peacock.

Below: Sir James Carroll.

Above: The Women's Christian Temperance Union wanted to stop all sales of alcohol.

Right: Kate Sheppard led the campaign for women to get the vote.

Votes for women

Kate Sheppard and the Women's Christian Temperance Union led a campaign to give women the same voting rights as men. In 1893 New Zealand became the first country in the world where women could vote. The Women's Christian Temperance Union was trying to stop the sale of alcohol in New Zealand. They wanted women to vote because they thought that women would support their cause. This turned out to be wrong. Women voted in much the same way as men.

Key points about political changes
- New Zealand used to be a colony and was ruled by Great Britain.
- It became an independent country gradually.
- The government is based on Great Britain's.
- We use MMP to elect our governments.
- Most citizens and permanent residents over 18 who live in New Zealand get to vote.

Left: Michael Joseph Savage was the first Labour prime minister — from 1935 to 1940. He was known as 'everybody's uncle' because he seemed so kind and friendly. He had an almost saint-like image.

Below: Helen Clark, the first elected woman prime minister — in 1999.

Below left: Jenny Shipley, the first woman prime minister. She gained control of a flagging National Government in 1997.

Above: Richard Seddon was called 'King Dick' and was prime minister from 1893 to 1906. He was the longest-serving prime minister. He had been a miner in Hokitika who went into local politics and was very popular. It was said that when he spoke to a crowd he played them like he was playing a piano.

Above: Robert Muldoon was prime minister from 1975 for nine years. He was famous for his 'Think Big' policies.

HOW WE ELECT A GOVERNMENT

Until 1995 New Zealand had an election system called First Past the Post or FPP. This meant that the party that won the most electorates formed the government. Sometimes a political party would get lots of votes over the whole country but not get enough seats to form a government. 'Not fair,' said some people.

A referendum was held in 1993, and as a result New Zealand introduced a new system. Under MMP (Mixed Member Proportional representation) each member of parliament (MP) is elected either as an electorate MP or as a list MP.

The voters cast two votes. The electorate vote is for the candidate the voter wants to represent his or her area in parliament. In the next election, probably in 2005, there will be 69 electorates. The party vote is for a political party rather than a candidate. The total number of party votes decides how many of the 120 seats in parliament each party will have. Extra members are added from a list of candidates published by the parties before the election.

Under this system the country is more likely to have coalition governments, where two or more political parties work together to form a government.

Changing ways of earning a living

FARMING

Some settlers worked for wages building roads or railways until they could buy a small piece of land. On 8 to 12 hectares they could grow vegetables and graze a cow.

Others were sheep farmers with big estates covering hundreds of hectares. They lived in very large houses, employed cooks, housemaids, nursemaids, other domestic servants, shepherds and farm workers. Their children were sent to private schools and studied in England. The wool was sold overseas. Unlike meat, it would not rot on the long sea voyage to Europe.

New Zealand, as a country of little farms and very big farms, began to change. The price of wool dropped during the 1890s. The huge farms could not pay their way. Other changes made middle-sized farms more profitable.

Above: Building the North Island Main Trunk Railway provided jobs for many settlers.

Below: Huge flocks of sheep produced wool for the overseas market.

Refrigerated cargo

People found out how to keep meat frozen on the long trip to Europe. The *Dunedin* left Port Chalmers and arrived in London 98 days later. It was a sailing ship with the machinery for keeping the meat frozen. But cinders from the boilers kept burning holes in the sails. The captain was worried the masts would burn down. The meat arrived in good condition and was sold for sixpence ha'penny a pound. It was a good price.

Farm division

Now that butter and cheese, as well as frozen meat, could be transported around the world, small farmers wanted more land for dairy

Below: With the growth of international trade, Auckland's wharves became busier.

Above: In 1882 the *Dunedin* carried the first cargo of frozen meat from New Zealand to Britain.

farms. The government helped by buying up large estates and splitting them up into medium-sized farms. Other big farmers decided to sell their land as well. The government lent money cheaply to new farmers to get started.

The family farm

The family farm earning its keep from dairying became common. New butter and cheese factories were set up. Most farmers did a bit of everything. They had dairy cows, they fattened lambs and they sheared wool. From 1900 to 1920 the average family farm was about 40 hectares in size. Horses pulled the machines. Cows were milked by hand.

Technological advances

Milking machines — first running on petrol, then, from the 1920s, on electricity — allowed farmers to have more cows. By 1919 nearly half the herds were milked using machines. By 1950 it was all the herds.

In the 1920s and 1930s science began to make a big difference to farming. Butterfat testing and better breeding techniques

Above left: Neighbours helped with threshing or haymaking.

Above: By the 1920s milking machines made work easier on dairy farms.

allowed farmers to raise the best cows for producing milk. By 1929 each cow on a dairy farm produced 72% more milk than a cow in 1901. Herd sizes grew from 50 or 60 just after World War II to an average of about 250 today, with some herds of 400 or more.

Soil scientists gave advice on the best grasses to grow. Top dressing with fertiliser improved the grass. Farmers did not have to

Below: Wives and children worked hard on the farm. The animals that they looked after usually ended up as dinner for the family.

Above: By 1950 tractors were becoming common on farms. Carey Sanson, aged 14, is on his dad's new tractor, a 1945 Farmall H.

re-sow their fields every year. More machinery was made and invented. Roads improved. It was easier to get the milk to the dairy factories, or the animals to the meat works.

INDUSTRY

Some people in towns worked long hours in small factories. The factories were often overcrowded, poorly lit and stuffy. The machinery did not have safety guards. Some boys and girls being trained on the job worked for almost nothing.

Clothing workers, working at home, were very badly paid. Cooks and domestic workers worked very long hours for low rates of pay. They had almost no time off, perhaps one Sunday a month.

New rules

After 1890 new laws were made. In factories there were strict rules about ventilation, safety and space. Working hours were shortened. Conditions at work were improved. For example, shop girls had to have a seat provided so they did not have to stand up for hours and hours. Workers had to be paid a minimum wage.

Unions helped to make sure conditions and wages were not unfair. Sometimes there were big strikes, such as Waihi in 1912, and the watersiders in 1913 and the 1951 lockout. At times workers found it better to use their votes and work through a political party to improve conditions.

New industries

Some people worked in coal mining, some in the timber industry. When native timber started to run out big plantations of exotics (trees not native to New Zealand like *Pinus*

Above: Buckle St in Wellington was the scene of this large protest during the Waterfront Strike in 1913.

Below: This man was injured at work. This issue has always concerned New Zealanders and led to many laws about safety at work. The Accident Compensation Corporation helps people who have suffered through accident.

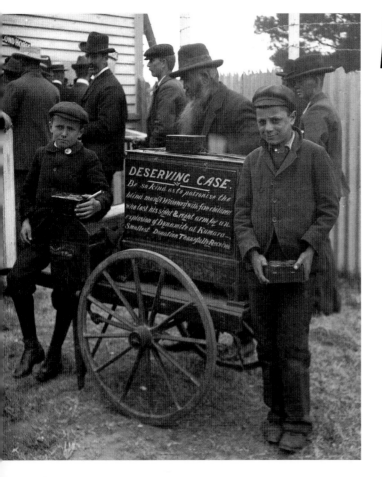

Above: New Zealand has been a popular tourist destination since the early 1900s.

radiata) were planted. New industries developed, like kiwifruit production and deer farming. Lots of New Zealanders have worked in tourism. The Pink and White Terraces, Rotorua with its mineral pools and geysers, Milford Sound and Aoraki (Mount Cook) were popular with early visitors. Maori guides like Rangi and Sophia showed visitors through the thermal wonders of Rotorua.

WOMEN AT WORK

Early settler women worked at home. They had more children. It was a full-time job to bake the bread, to keep the family fed, clothed and healthy. But as families became smaller and electricity provided washing machines,

Above: The great kauri forests of Northland provided excellent building timber.

electric stoves and refrigerators, more women got paid jobs.

After 1884 married women were allowed to keep their own wages. They did not have to hand them over to their husbands. Early on most women found jobs as domestic workers, teachers or nurses. They were paid less than men even if they were doing the same job. Most preferred working in factories to being domestic workers. They had more independence and freedom.

By the 1920s most women worked before they married. Being a typist or a telephone operator was much better than being a servant. A few women became doctors or lawyers.

During the wars, with men away fighting, many women worked in 'men's' jobs. After this it was possible for women to move into a wide range of occupations. After the 1960s women had to be paid as much as men to do the same work.

Below: Ethel Benjamin became a lawyer in 1897.

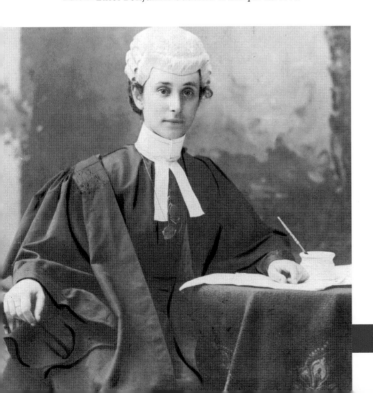

Key points about earning a living

- Growing food and raising animals has been very important in earning a living in New Zealand.
- New Zealanders have earned a living from many varied occupations — from gold mining to kiwifruit growing.
- Conditions and wages have been important issues for workers.
- Women steadily moved into paid employment outside the home.

Fighting outside New Zealand

Above: Men and horses ready to leave for South Africa.

SOUTH AFRICAN WAR

This war was between the British and the Boers (South Africans of Dutch descent) from 1899 to 1902. New Zealand, as a loyal member of the British Empire, sent 10 contingents of volunteers — 6500 men and 8000 horses. The British paid most of the costs. This was New Zealand's first overseas war and many men were keen to sign up. A small group of women went as nurses. Of the New Zealanders, 228 died. More died from disease than from fighting. The horses were left behind when the soldiers went home.

WORLD WAR I

This war, from 1914 to 1918, was called the Great War — people thought at the time it was the war to end all wars. New Zealand fought alongside Britain and her allies. The aim was to control the expansion of Germany and her allies.

Right: New Zealanders landing on the beach at Gallipoli.

Remembrance

The red poppy is the symbol adopted to remember those who died in war. In the fields of Northern France and Belgium, where many of the worst battles of World War I were fought, the wild red poppy flowers in spring remind people of the soldiers who shed blood in those fields.

Gallipoli

ANZAC stands for Australia and New Zealand Army Corps. It was an army division formed in Egypt before the landing at Gallipoli. The word now symbolises the friendship between Australia and New Zealand.

On 25 April 1915 Anzac troops landed on Gallipoli peninsula in Turkey. It was a hopeless fight. The New Zealanders captured the hilltop of Chunuk Bair. Many died, some killed by British fire. The hilltop was re-occupied by the Turks shortly afterwards. Nearly 3000 New Zealanders died at Gallipoli and 4752 were wounded. Many of the

Above: Te Moananui-a-Kiwa Ngarimu earned a Victoria Cross for his bravery in World War II.

Above: The Maori Battalion were fierce fighters in World War II. This group of Maori Battalion soldiers are leaving Rotorua to go to war.

wounded died later from their wounds.

The whole campaign had been a big mistake. Ever since, New Zealand and Australia have kept 25 April as a special day of mourning for those killed in war.

Belgium and France

New Zealanders also fought in Belgium and in Northern France. Nearly 50,000 were killed or wounded fighting in the trenches amid the mud and the gas attacks. Many more men from New Zealand were killed in World War I than in later wars. Every New Zealand town built war memorials listing the names of those who died.

WORLD WAR II

This was a war against fascism. New Zealand fought with the other democracies against Hitler's Germany, Mussolini's Italy, and Japan. When Britain declared war on Germany, New Zealand's prime minister, Michael Joseph Savage, said, 'Where Britain goes we go.' Actually, because our time is 12 hours ahead of Britain, we declared war on Germany before Britain did.

Where did New Zealanders fight?

The New Zealand Division fought in the deserts of North Africa against the Germans and Italians. They tried unsuccessfully to save Greece and Crete from German invasion. They were led by Major-General Bernard Freyberg. After 1943, when the Germans had been beaten in North Africa, the New Zealanders fought in Italy. They were involved in the Battle of Cassino. New Zealanders also fought in the Pacific, and New Zealand fighter pilots flew in the Battle of Britain.

Casualties

In the war cemeteries of Europe there are rows and rows of crosses marking the graves of New Zealanders who came from everywhere from Bluff to Taihape, from Taihape to Kaitaia. Many were young men of no more than 18 or 20 who had never been overseas before. All in all, in World War II 11,600 New Zealanders died and more than 15,000 were wounded.

Maori Battalion

More than 17,000 Maori fought in World War II, many of them in the famous Maori Battalion feared by the Germans and Italians for their fierce fighting. Te Moananui-a-Kiwa Ngarimu, of Ngati Porou, earned the Victoria Cross for bravery. He was killed in action.

Left and above: Because the men were away fighting the war, women took over a lot of their jobs.

Pacific war

Japan invaded the Pacific and New Zealand was under threat. But the Japanese were beaten in naval battles by the United States navy. Thousands of American soldiers and marines came to New Zealand. Eventually two atomic bombs dropped on Japan by the United States in 1945 forced Japan to surrender.

Conscription

New Zealand had conscription. All young healthy men of 18 or more who were not needed for important work at home had to join the army. Women too were conscripted to work in New Zealand so that men could be freed up to fight.

At home

War took over our lives. Petrol and rubber and some foods such as butter and pork were rationed. Car tyres were not replaced but

Right: Some people refused to fight no matter what happened. All sorts of people were conscientious objectors — the peacetime occupations of the men pictured at this camp in Hautu were lawyer, labourer, waterside worker, clerk, social worker and pig farmer.

mended again and again. Children practised air-raid drills and were issued with gas masks at school.

But no one in New Zealand went hungry. Food was rationed only so we could send food to Britain. At the end of the war we were one of the few countries without big debts, because everyone was so keen to buy our food.

Above: Devonport school pupils and teachers entering air-raid shelters during World War II.

CONFLICT IN ASIA

Korean War

When North Korea invaded South Korea in 1950, New Zealand was part of the United Nations effort to assist South Korea. Artillery, drivers, signallers, engineers and frigates —

but not infantry — were sent. By the time the war ended in 1953, 33 New Zealanders had been killed.

Vietnam War

Many New Zealanders opposed sending troops to support the American intervention in a civil war in Vietnam in the mid-1960s. Only a small contingent of New Zealanders went. In 1972–73 the war ended with an American defeat.

Right: New Zealand has been a strong supporter of the United Nations and our soldiers have been sent as peace-keepers to places like the Middle East, Cyprus and East Timor and Bougainville.

Key points about fighting overseas

- New Zealanders — both men and women — have played an important role in overseas wars.
- Many have lost their lives in the service of their country.
- People at home played their part too.
- War affected everyone's lives.

Bad times and the role of the government

By the 1870s the wars in New Zealand were over. In the North Island progress had been held back. The richer South Island saw gold running out. People decided to go to Australia to live. Few new settlers came.

Above: Early roads were in very bad condition. Better roads needed to be built.

It was difficult to get from one settlement to another. People had to travel by sea. There were few roads. No one was rich enough to build the roads, bridges and railways the country needed.

THE DEPRESSION OF THE 1880S

Julius Vogel had worked on the gold fields and then founded the *Otago Daily Times*, the first daily paper. He went into politics.

Vogel became very influential in the government. In 1870 he put a new idea before the people. It was like a bombshell. He said they

Left: As Prime Minister, Julius Vogel borrowed a lot of money so New Zealand could build roads and railways.

Above: Over 100,000 new settlers, mostly families, came to New Zealand in the following years under Vogel's scheme.

Above: Road building was tough work. These men are building a road as part of a government scheme during the depression in the 1930s.

could borrow money as a country to spend on roads and railways. They could borrow *big* — £6 million. And the country could pay for more people to come to New Zealand. It could pay their fares and they would work hard and pay the money back in taxes. Vogel's idea was that the government should do what individual people were not rich enough to do — develop the country. Over 100,000 new settlers arrived, and new roads and railways were built.

Problems

But there were difficulties. Paying the borrowed money back was hard. The wool New Zealand was selling overseas did not make enough money. It was worth less each year. There were not enough jobs for people. Some wandered from farm to farm with their swags looking for work. Businesses collapsed. Farmers could not afford to improve their farms. Some lost them when they could not repay loans. This time was called 'the long depression' and lasted from the late 1870s to 1895.

Help for the poor

In 1890 the Liberals won the election. They stayed in power for the next 20 years. People thought it was the job of the government to do something to help end the depression. New laws broke up big farms, helped new farmers with cheap loans, and improved working conditions in factories.

Many old pioneers had worked all their lives clearing the bush or making roads. They had no families to help them and had not saved any money. Up till then people thought families should look after poor and sick people. In New Zealand, churches were not rich enough to help.

In 1898 a new law was made giving old people a small pension — 6 shillings 11 pence a week. It was enough to keep them alive if they grew their own vegetables and kept chickens. Later the government also helped widows, built some cheap houses, provided a few free places in secondary schools and set up free maternity hospitals. But it was a new idea that the government should help ordinary people when they were in trouble.

After 1895 overseas prices improved, and new products like butter, cheese and frozen meat could be sold. Times got better.

THE DEPRESSION OF THE 1930S

Another big depression began in the 1920s when overseas prices for our products went up and down — but mostly down. Many people lost their jobs. By 1929, 6000 people were out of work. By 1930, 11,000 were out of work.

Food prices went up. Housing was expensive so families crowded into old homes. Sickness and disease spread easily. People could not afford to go to hospital or see a doctor. Many children did not get enough to eat. Children were dressed in clothes made from flour sacks, shoes had cardboard inside to patch up their soles, old jerseys were unpicked to be reknitted.

To help, the Liberal government paid men a tiny wage to work on building roads or planting trees. The worst unemployment was in 1932–33. In Dunedin, Wellington and Auckland the people were so angry that there were riots. They smashed windows and looted shops.

Below: These young boys cut and packed kindling to help earn some money for their families.

Social security

In the 1935 election, people wanted change and voted in the Labour Party. The new government took up the idea that it should look after those who were in trouble. This new idea was called 'social security'. The

Left: During the depression in the 1930s a lot of people relied on charity organisations to help them. This queue of people is waiting outside the Smith Family Joyspreaders in Wellington.

Below: People wanted change. Crowds of unemployed workers went to Parliament to protest.

government introduced better pensions, free health programmes and education. New state houses were built and people could borrow money to build their own.

HAPPIER TIMES

Luckily, prices for our exports started to improve and New Zealand gradually recovered. From the end of the 1940s until the late 1960s New Zealand was quite prosperous. The world was eager to pay good prices for our meat, dairy products and wool.

Above: Michael Joseph Savage, the leader of the Labour Party, was called 'everybody's uncle' because he seemed so friendly. He even helped these people move the furniture into their new state house.

People were out of work. Some left for Australia. Governments borrowed money from overseas. New Zealand got more into debt and things got worse.

Big changes

Between 1984 and 1992 a new Labour government introduced big changes. Many of the government controls were swept away. The government no longer controlled the exchange rate of the New Zealand dollar. Shopping hours were extended. Farmers lost their subsidies on things like fertilisers.

The Labour government asked if it was necessary for the state to own railways, airlines, forests and the telephone system. Earlier in our history it had been because no individuals were rich enough. The number of government workers was reduced. Government debt fell and there was a rise in the number of jobs. But this economic restructuring was very hurtful, especially to small communities that lost their post offices or their community hospitals.

Above: State houses were built for people who couldn't afford to buy their own homes.

Government control

But we had strict laws too. There was no shopping at the weekends, no spending too much money if you went overseas. No importing too many cars. Farmers were given subsidies to buy fertiliser. There was lots of government control and protection of industries from overseas competition.

But in the 1970s the price of petrol and oil went up and our exports were worth less.

Above: Cutbacks to hospital services on Auckland's North Shore brought these people out to protest against the government in 1989.

Left: Police and protesters clash near Eden Park during the Springbok Tour protests in 1981.

Left: In 1982, people protested against Prime Minister Robert Muldoon's tax reforms.

Key points about bad times

- New Zealand's wealth depends on selling our goods overseas for a good price.
- We expect the government to help out if things go wrong.

Disasters

New Zealand's worst disaster happened in 1979. An Air New Zealand DC10 crashed into Mount Erebus in Antarctica, killing all 257 people on board.

Severe storms sometimes affect New Zealand. On 10 April 1968 a severe storm with freak gale-force winds blew the inter-island ferry *Wahine* off course. She hit Barretts Reef in Wellington Harbour and 51 people drowned.

EARTHQUAKES

Earthquakes happen often in New Zealand. Large, shallow ones do most damage.

Wellington

The first settlement in Wellington had only just begun, when in 1848 a series of heavy shocks destroyed parts of the town. The settlers were terrified and many left the area.

In 1855 came New Zealand's biggest

Above: In 1979, an Air New Zealand plane crashed into Mount Erebus in Antarctica. This was New Zealand's worst disaster.

Below: The *Wahine* just before she sank in Wellington Harbour.

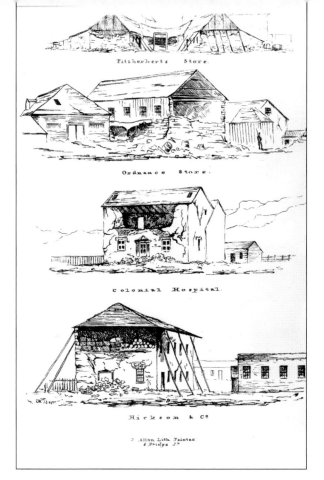

Above: The big earthquake at Murchison caused the slip that destroyed this house.

Left: An earthquake in Wellington in 1855 caused major damage to these buildings.

recorded earthquake, felt on both sides of Cook Strait. It killed 12 people and lifted up land in the Hutt Valley.

Murchison

Seventeen people died in 1929 when the Murchison earthquake created big land slips. The small settlement was wiped out. The survivors said that during the worst jolt they could not stand upright.

Napier

In 1931 Napier had a series of earthquakes. They began on 3 February late in the morning. In the earthquakes 256 people were killed and 3600 hectares of land was thrust upwards. It razed the town of Napier and shattered Hastings.

There have been other earthquakes too at Inangahua and Edgecumbe.

Below: Hastings St in Napier after the huge 1931 Hawke's Bay earthquake. This quake caused so much damage that most of Napier had to be rebuilt.

VOLCANOES

Mount Tarawera

The Pink and White Terraces on the shores of Lake Rotomahana were a great tourist attraction. Some said that they were one of the wonders of the world. But in June 1886 Mount Tarawera erupted on the eastern side of the lake. Three craters on the mountain were destroyed. The eruption covered the Pink and

Above: The Pink and White Terraces at Rotomahana were destroyed when Mt Tarawera erupted in 1886.

White Terraces with lava and drained Lake Rotomahana, though it refilled later. The ash from the eruption was flung over thousands of square kilometres of forest and farmland. The three Maori villages of Te Wairoa, Te Ariki and Moura were destroyed, and 153 people were killed.

Below: Sheltering in this chicken coop saved these men's lives in the Tarawera eruption.

Mount Ruapehu

Mount Ruapehu is an active volcano and the ski fields have sometimes had to be closed because of danger from eruptions. It has a large crater lake. On Christmas Eve 1953 the lake burst through the wall of the crater. A powerful lahar, a flood of mud and silt, roared down the Whangaehu River. It destroyed a railway bridge just before the Wellington to Auckland night express arrived.

A man tried to warn the train driver by running up the track waving a light and shouting, but the driver could not stop in time. The first five carriages and the engine plunged into the swollen river and 151 people died. After that a warning system was set up in case the crater lake burst its banks again.

Rangitoto

The most recent volcanic eruption in Auckland was Rangitoto. It happened about 600 years ago. We know Maori were already in Auckland and witnessed the eruption. Archaeologists have found footprints in the now hard, but then soft, volcanic ash. Strangely enough, there are no known legends about the volcanic eruption, though it must have been very dramatic. Perhaps the stories died out when people were killed in warfare or died from disease.

Above: 151 people were killed when this train plunged into the river at Tangiwai on Christmas Eve, 1953.

Below right: Mt Ruapehu erupted again in 1995. This time it didn't cause nearly as much damage as it did in 1953.

Below: The dramatic eruption of Mt Tarawera on June 10, 1886. This painting is by Charles Blomfield.

Changes in our lives

If your great-great-grandparents could see you now what would surprise them? Here are some of the questions they might ask.

How many people live in New Zealand now?

There were between 80,000 and 200,000 Maori living in New Zealand when Captain Cook arrived in 1762. By 1858–59 there were equal numbers of Maori and Pakeha — about 115,000 altogether. In 1910 the population was up to 1 million. In 1952 we hit 2 million. By 1973 the population had increased to 3 million. And in 2003 it was 4 million.

Just where in New Zealand do they live?

In the very early days most lived in the north, in the Bay of Islands. Then new settlers came to Canterbury, Otago, Nelson, Wellington, Taranaki and Auckland. When gold was discovered the rush was to the south. Then in the early 20th century people moved northwards again. By the mid-1990s one-third of the population of New Zealand lived in the greater urban area of Auckland, more than in the whole of the South Island.

Where have people come from?

Maori came from the eastern Pacific. Most 19th-century settlers came from England, Scotland, Wales and Ireland. Many came via Australia. Small numbers came from European countries like Poland, Italy, Denmark and Bohemia. Polynesians from Pacific Islands like Samoa, Niue and Tonga came in the mid-20th century. After the 1980s more new citizens

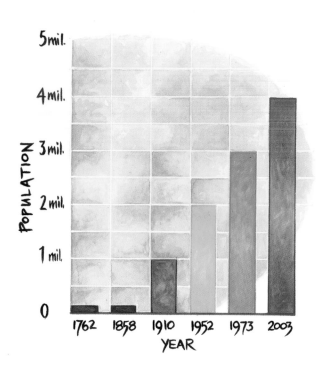

Above: In 240 years New Zealand's population has grown enormously.

arrived from Hong Kong, Taiwan, China, Korea and other Asian countries.

Do people still live on small farms in the countryside?

By 1926 nearly 60% of the population lived in towns. The cities began to spread out. With the arrival of the car in the early 20th century, suburbs grew along the main roads. You no longer had to live near where you worked. You did not have to shop close to home either. The supermarket, the video store, the shopping mall would all be strange to your great-great-grandmother.

Does your family still cook using wood or coal as fuel?

With electricity becoming available in the 1920s people's lives changed. Electric lights, household gadgets, telephones, radios and movies became part of everyone's lives.

Left: After World War II many new immigrants came from Europe.

Below left: Many Polynesian families have settled in New Zealand.

Do people still write letters to each other?

In the 1920s the telephone became widespread. Computers and email began to change our ways of communicating from the 1980s. Cellphones became popular in the 1990s. There have been big changes in the way we send messages to each other, in our shopping and the way we work.

Do children go to school regularly?

When the pioneer European settlers arrived, most children worked all day on the family farm. Parents needed their labour and could not afford the cost of schooling. In towns it was easier to send children to school. But because education was seen as important, settlers soon set up schools. Ideas about children were changing. People felt that they should lead a more protected childhood. They felt children

Below: With the arrival of the motor car you did not have to work or shop close to where you lived.

Right: Electricity and washing machines made housework much easier.

Below: The telephone was very important for improving communications.

should not have to work hard all day but have time to learn to play the piano, or just to play. Children should be able to go to school and not be beaten at home or at school.

In 1877 attending primary school was made compulsory and free. Most students left school when they finished standard 6 (year 8). In Maori communities parents provided land and part of the teachers' pay. The government paid the rest. Teaching was in English, usually with a Pakeha teacher.

By the 1890s every district had a school, often with a horse paddock. Many students had to ride to school over a rough track. Classes were large and discipline was strict.

Secondary schooling did not become free and compulsory until after World War II. In 1944 secondary education to 15 was made compulsory. The government had to build many more secondary schools. In 1995 the school leaving age was raised to 16.

Universities were established after 1869. Otago was the first and others followed soon after.

Are families as large as they used to be?

Families have been getting smaller. In our great-great-grandparents' time families often had six or seven children. But some would die before they were five years old. Now fewer children are born, perhaps two or less per family but also fewer die young. Our health services have improved and organisations like the Plunket Society, established by Sir Truby King, have helped. He set up special hospitals for babies and taught mothers how to care for their babies. The aim was to have healthy babies.

Is the family structure the same?

Most families are still mother, father and children with other relatives nearby. But we have a greater variety of types of family than in the past.

We have more solo parents. There were always widows or widowers with children.

Below: Foxton School. Going to school was free and compulsory after 1877.

Above: Universities were established. The first one was Otago.

Below: The Irving family of Reefton in the 1890s had six children.

There were always people who had been deserted by their partners. Until the 1980s divorce was not possible just because people were not happy together — there had to be serious problems. It was expensive and easier for men than for women. It was a very shameful process with names appearing in the newspaper, as well as the reasons for the divorce. Since 1980 divorce has been a private matter, and the same for men and women.

Above: The Plunket Society helped mothers raise healthy babies by keeping a record of their progress in books like this.

Above: In the 1920s movies were silent and black and white.

In our great-great-grandparents' time what went on in the home was seen as private business. Even if there was violence, married couples were expected to stay together. Now we do not expect people to stay in a marriage or a partnership if there is violence. Society has decided it is better to give solo parents financial support.

But perhaps the biggest change in the family has been to teenagers. They were ignored before the 1950s. Then advertisers began to appeal to the teenage market. Teenagers were seen to have their own style, with distinctive clothes, their own music and even some of their own language.

How do people enjoy themselves?

Sports became much more organised in the 1890s, with rules instead of a free-for-all. Movie theatres were built in the 1920s for silent, black-

and-white movies. After 1929 the 'talkies' hit the screen. The car made everyone much more mobile. By 1937 there was one vehicle for every seven people, by 1981 one vehicle for every two people. Television was introduced in 1960 and was widespread by the late 1970s. Being able to show a video at home made many movie theatres close down. By 1981, 67%

Below: Television has become an extremely popular pastime. TV stars are celebrities.

Above: Television programmes like *Being Eve* are specifically targeted at teenagers.

of the population had colour television sets. New recreations such as bungy jumping, windsurfing or skateboarding would be very strange to your great-great-grandparents. And as for going to the gym instead of clearing the land or doing the washing by hand, that they would never understand.

And has money changed?

In 1967 decimal coinage replaced pounds, shillings and pence. The new dollar was the equivalent of 10 shillings.

Far right: Teenagers have developed their own sports like skateboarding.

Right: The half-penny, penny and half-crown have all been replaced. Recently the one and two cent coins disappeared.

Changes in Maori lives

At the end of the 19th century 95% of Maori lived in the country. They lived apart from the Pakeha. The population was down to 42,000 by 1896 mostly because of sickness. In the 20th century the death rate dropped and numbers began to increase.

Above: A Maori woman weaving a mat from flax. Most Maori still lived in country areas.

Below left: With the sittings of the Native Land Court, much Maori land had been sold. This photograph shows a crowd gathered at Ahipara on Maori Land Court day.

A TIME FOR LEADERS

Tribal loyalties were very important. Leaders were coming forward who felt comfortable in Maori and in Pakeha ways. Schools had been built in Maori villages. Parents were keen for their children to learn. New churches, which combined old ideas with Christian ideas, provided a sense of belonging.

Above: Wiremu Ratana founded the Ratana Church in the Whanganui area. This new church appealed to many from different tribes. The Ratana movement allied with the Labour Party to provide a strong voice for Maori.

Above: Rua Kenana (right) of Tuhoe built a settlement in the Urewera based upon a religion. But because he opposed conscription during World War I he was distrusted. The police arrested him, using an excuse that he was selling alcohol without a licence. His settlement was never as strong again.

Left: Princess Te Puea, great-granddaughter of King Potatau te Wherowhero, worked hard to rebuild Ngaruawahia as the centre of the Maori King Movement.

LAND ISSUES

From the 1930s on there was more government help in housing, health, and reorganising the land. Maori people began to move to the towns (by 1990 most Maori lived in towns). More went on to higher education. There were lots of marriages between Maori and Pakeha people.

But there were issues that worried Maori leaders. The Treaty of Waitangi had never been taken very seriously by Pakeha. Maori felt that their taonga (precious things) were in danger. These taonga were land, fishing rights, language and customs. In 1975 there was a land march from the far north to parliament to highlight land issues.

WAITANGI TRIBUNAL

In 1975 a special tribunal was set up to hear grievances and advise the government on what to do about land issues. It was called the Waitangi Tribunal. Many claims were registered. Some claims, such as that of Ngai Tahu, have been settled. Bastion Point was returned to Ngati Whatua as part of their settlement.

Maori language has been promoted by setting up schools and kindergartens teaching in Maori. These are called kohanga reo and kura kaupapa Maori. A Maori television channel has been set up.

Above: Dame Whina Cooper was a prominent leader for over 60 years. In 1975, she led a land rights march, or hikoi, from the far north all the way to parliament in Wellington. She became known as Whaea O Te Motu — Mother of the Nation.

Key points about Maori life
- Most Maori now live in the towns.
- Maori population has increased steadily since 1900.
- Maori churches and organisations have provided a focus for Maori language and culture.
- The Waitangi Tribunal is trying to work out a partnership between Pakeha and Maori.

Right: Sir Apirana Ngata of Ngati Porou was at home in both Maori and Pakeha worlds. He became a doctor, then a cabinet minister. He helped in Maori health and farming.

Above: Te Whiti set up a strongly pacifist (they believed in non-violence) village, Parihaka, in southern Taranaki in the 1870s. His people ploughed up land which had been confiscated from the Taranaki people. The government was unhappy about his independent stand. They sent in troops to destroy the village and arrest Te Whiti.

Right: Maori protesters occupied tribal lands which had been taken unfairly. Bastion Point in Auckland was the scene of one of the biggest protests.

Below: The land march, or hikoi, highlighted land issues and brought them to the attention of parliament.

Some of our heroes and heroines

Charles Upham (1908–1994)

An outstanding soldier, he won the Victoria Cross twice for bravery in World War II. He was very daring and very determined. He ended the war in a prison camp called Colditz Castle.

1905 All Blacks

A New Zealand touring rugby team in Britain with an outstanding record of victories, they were so fast that one commentator said that they must be all backs. It was misprinted as 'all blacks'. Ever since then the New Zealand rugby team has been called the All Blacks.

Lord Ernest Rutherford (1871–1937)

He was a famous international scientist who grew up in Nelson. He went to England and became head of the well-known Cavendish research laboratory. His work in nuclear physics laid the basis for the science. He showed how the atom is structured, discovered the laws of radioactivity, and was the first person to split the nucleus of the atom. Without his understanding of the structure of the atom, there would be no modern electronics industry.

Sir Edmund Hillary (b. 1919)

In 1953, with Sherpa Tenzing Norgay, Hillary climbed the world's highest peak, Mount Everest in the Himalayas. They were the first men to do so. Hillary also led an expedition to the Antarctic.

Jean Batten (1909–1982)

She was the most famous New Zealander of the 1930s. A world-famous aviatrix (the old name for a female pilot), she made solo flights from England to India and Brazil. In 1936, at the age of 26, she broke the record for a solo flight from England to Australia (21 hours) and then crossed the Tasman (9¼ hours).

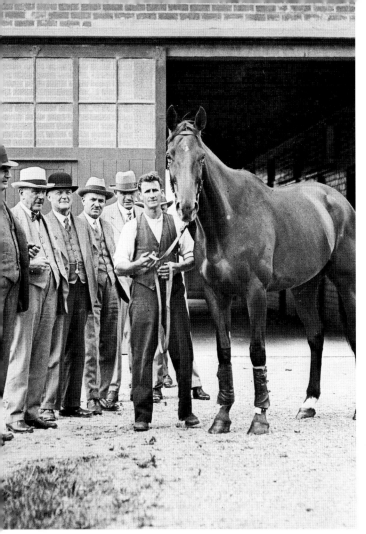

Phar Lap

Phar Lap was probably the best racehorse New Zealand has ever produced. A big red horse, he was a galloper and raced in Australia in the early 1930s. He was phenomenally successful. He was taken to Mexico to race in the richest race in North America. He won the race in a record time but died three weeks later of a mysterious illness.

Katherine Mansfield (1883–1923)

Perhaps New Zealand's most famous writer, she left New Zealand and lived in Britain and France. She is known as one of the world's best short-story writers.

Below: The 1905 All Blacks.

Pelorus Jack and Opo

For 25 years Pelorus Jack, a dolphin, accompanied ships travelling between Nelson and Wellington. He would play around the bow of the ship. He did this regularly between 1888 and 1912, when he disappeared. Tourists loved him. The government passed a special law protecting him in 1904.

Opo, another dolphin, had a much shorter career. In 1955 and 1956 she played with swimmers at Opononi in the Hokianga Harbour. She would even allow some children to climb on her back. She, too, was given personal protection as her fame increased but she was found dead, stranded in a rock pool.

Above: Pelorus Jack.

Right: Opo.

Sir Peter Blake (1948–2001)

He was a famous sailor who sailed the Whitbread Round the World Race. He organised the team that won the America's Cup in 1995 and defended it successfully in 2000. He was murdered while doing environmental work in South America.

Professor Fred Hollows (1929–1993)

He became known internationally for pioneering the treatment of eye disease among Australian aborigines, and in developing countries. The Fred Hollows Foundation continues his work today in more than 29 countries. They have already helped over a million people to see again.

Janet Frame (1924–2004)

She is the best-known novelist New Zealand has produced, and has an international reputation.

Peter Jackson (b. 1961)

He has made his reputation as a film writer and director.

Dame Kiri Te Kanawa (b. 1944)

She is New Zealand's best-known opera singer. She has based her international career in London.

His best-known films are the *Lord of the Rings* series, filmed in New Zealand. The picture at right shows Peter Jackson with two of the stars of *Heavenly Creatures*.

How has human occupation affected New Zealand?

After 1000 to 1500 years we have changed the face of the land. It is now mostly grass or cropland, not forest. Both Maori and Pakeha burnt off the forest. Some of the forest cover we now have is exotic forest like pinus radiata.

EXTINCTION

Some species of plants and animals have adapted to the change. Others have disappeared. Some 20 species of birds disappeared after Maori arrived. With the clearing of the bush and the farming by the Pakeha many more species lost their habitats and disappeared. We have to work hard to preserve threatened species such as the tuatara, the Chatham Island robin, the takahe and many more.

Right: These are some of the farms on the Canterbury Plains.

Below: The *Pinus radiata* is now one of the most common trees in New Zealand.

Above: The takahe was once thought to be extinct. It is one of our rarest birds.

PESTS

We have introduced some nasty imports. Maori introduced kiore and the dog, which killed many birds. Pakeha introduced red deer for hunting, and animals like Australian possums which were considered interesting, exotic animals. Rabbits, stoats, weasels and ferrets came. Norwegian rats arrived as stowaways. These have harmed the environment, breeding rapidly in a land without predators. More recently we have had the varroa mite attacking bees.

We have tried to eradicate some very nasty imports rather than just keep them under control. There were campaigns to eradicate the gypsy moth from the eastern suburbs of Auckland, and the painted apple moth from the western suburbs of Auckland.

But don't forget we have also imported all sorts of useful plants and animals in order to make a living. We have a great variety of animal and plant life. We also have a great variety of people and cultures in our human population of 4 million!

Below: The stoat is one nasty import.

Below: Grapes have proved to be a very useful import as they are used to make wine.

Illustration credits

Index